What people are saying about …

ONE WAY LOVE

"I have been greatly encouraged by the emergence of a new generation of committed and articulate Christian leaders—and my grandson Tullian Tchividjian is certainly at the forefront of this development. His deep understanding of the Gospel and his unique ability to communicate its timeless truths with compassion and insight have already had a profound impact on countless men and women. May God use this book to expand your understanding of what Jesus Christ has already done for you."

Billy Graham, evangelist and author
of *The Reason for My Hope*

"I could not stop reading this book. I could not stop thinking about this book. I could not stop returning to this book. I could not stop mouthing yes, yes, yes over every page. Tullian writes with profound insight, humbling transparency, biblical fidelity, and one surgically sharp pen that cuts away the infected areas and brings healing through the Word of Christ. Do not pass Go until you have read this book. It's like getting your life on a one-way street to everything you ever hoped for."

Ann Voskamp, author of the *New York Times* bestseller *One Thousand Gifts*

"Tullian goes straight to the heart of what is taking the heart out of people: an addiction to performance. Performancism equates value with accomplishments. God's grace, on the other hand, equates value with God's love. It is one-way, from Him. And it is guaranteed. Tullian captures the wonder of grace and offers it to us all. I urge you to read this book!"

Max Lucado, pastor and bestselling author

"My friend Tullian is a man on fire. He has one thing to say: Jesus came to set you free. This book will make you laugh and cry. But most importantly, it wonderfully points you to the only man and message that can lighten your load and bring you the rest you've been searching for your whole life."

Rick Warren, #1 *New York Times* bestselling author of *The Purpose Driven Life* and pastor of Saddleback Church

"It's possible that the church's inability to grasp the concept of God's grace has kept more people away from Jesus than anything else. What a tragedy! Will we ever understand something so radical—and even offensive? And yet we must. *One Way Love* by Tullian Tchividjian would be a perfect place to start."

Eric Metaxas, *New York Times* bestselling author of *Bonhoeffer* and *Amazing Grace*

"In the pressure-cooker world of professional sports that I live in, where it's tempting to locate my value in how I perform, Tullian's book comes as a relieving breath of fresh air."

Tony Romo, quarterback for the Dallas Cowboys

he now shares that unbridled, radical, and entirely free grace with others as he preaches the gospel of Jesus Christ. Get this book and discover what God's one-way love, His grace, truly looks like."

Mark Batterson, *New York Times*
bestselling author of *The Circle Maker*

"*One Way Love* is exactly what I need to be reading right now—wait, make that every day. Every single moment of every single day, I need to be reminded of the unexpected, startling, and inexhaustible grace of God for sinners like me. I'm so grateful to Tullian for this book."

Sally Lloyd-Jones, author of *The Jesus Storybook Bible* and *Thoughts to Make Your Heart Sing*

"Performance = fatigue. Grace = liberation. Let Tullian get you off your treadmill of endless work and stifling legalism so you can rest with confidence in God's great love for you. Here's an encouraging, insightful, and urgent call to be thoroughly free in Christ."

Lee Strobel, bestselling author of *The Case for Christ* and *The Case for Faith*

"What a wonderfully needed and personally restorative book. May it give rest and hope to a culture of exhausted Christians. May it help us face what we don't want to face—that we'll never ever measure up—and help us embrace what seems impossible—that God really does give us His best when we're at our worst. I suspect you're like me—tired of being tired. Well, if you are, this book is for you. There really is eternal love that you can't earn and boundless grace that only comes as a gift. As *One Way Love* anticipates our questions and speaks to our objections, it reminds us that, together, this love and grace offer us the rest our weary souls seek."

Paul Tripp, counselor and bestselling author

"Tullian faithfully contextualizes the gospel before a culture that wobbles between hedonism and moralism. This book speaks to the 'religious' and 'secular' moralists, identifying their common root—idolatrous self-empowerment. A strong read."

J. D. Greear, pastor of the Summit Church and author of *Stop Asking Jesus Into Your Heart* and *Gospel*

"A new book from Tullian Tchividjian is always a cause for celebration! I'm an old, cynical preacher, and sometimes I grow so tired—exhausted, really—from trying to live up to the standards of those who manipulate and manage in the name of Jesus. This book is like a safe harbor in a ghastly storm, because it's about truth, grace, and Jesus. *One Way Love: Inexhaustible Grace for an Exhausted World* is a refreshing drink of cold, pure water to a thirsty soul. Read it, and give it to everybody you know. They will rise up and call you blessed."

Steve Brown, president of Key Life Network, radio-show host, and author of *Three Free Sins*

"Tullian has a cut-and-thrust style that's completely engrossing. I was totally captured from the first sentence. His pearl of great price is God's therapy for our wounds. It's a therapy of no 'buts or brakes.' Haven't you had it with buts and brakes? As if the world doesn't crowd you with enough of them to stint any of life's joys, the church lards them on *sans merci*. 'Down with them,' says Tullian! But not for Tullian's sake, or for any man's or woman's sake, but down with them for Christ's sake. *One Way Love* should be a sing-along book. It should be a Coca-Cola jingle. It's the Real Thing. And this book will teach the world to sing."

Dr. Paul F. M. Zahl, author of *Grace in Practice*

"In One Way Love, Tullian pours the herbicide of grace on the deadly daisy of 'He loves me, He loves me not' spirituality. Through well-chosen episodes from God's story and revealing anecdotes from his own story, my friend invites us to consider the radical implications of the only love that is better than life, the only love that will never let go of us, the only love that is one way—God's unilateral and unwavering, immeasurable and irrepressible love for us in Jesus. Performance-based Christianity and self-fixated discipleship just got served notice. God's love alone is compelling enough to help us get over ourselves and into God's purposes."

Scotty Smith, founding pastor of
Christ Community Church

"Tullian is obsessed with grace—in a good way. He knows (and most of us know) that we are saved by grace, but Tullian does not want us to get over it—he wants us to live by grace. In *One Way Love*, Tullian goes at the heart of something that I (and probably you, too) struggle with—being driven by performance rather than by the grace of God. Let this book speak to your performance addiction and draw you more deeply into God's grace."

Ed Stetzer, president of LifeWay Research

"In One Way Love, Tullian Tchividjian's words read like a truth-arrow shot straight from the heart of God—a God whose extravagant love moves one way toward us without disclaimers, asterisks, or fine print. Weaving Tullian's personal story together with the deep theology of grace, this book is one of the most comprehensive explanations of the gospel I have ever read."

Emily P. Freeman, author of *A Million Little Ways* and *Grace for the Good Girl*

"IT'S NOT ABOUT WHAT YOU DO OR WHAT YOU'VE DONE! What a novel concept! *One Way Love* is one of the most important books to come out in a long time. Resting in this truth will set you free: no matter what you do—good or bad—it is not possible for Christ to love you any more than He already does. This book has been a hard reset in the way I see grace, and things will be different from here on out."

Bart Millard, lead singer of MercyMe

"Tchividjian has done it again. His books have a compelling predictability to them: raw and honest biblical realism skillfully interwoven with equally candid threads from his life's story, yielding a rich tapestry of grace in motion. One-way love, indeed. This book takes the reader on an enthralling journey into the depths of the profound love of God in Christ and its immeasurable greatness in the lives of His beloved children. Do-it-yourselfers and spiritual wannabes beware: Tullian will drown your misbeliefs in a tsunami of God's radical love."

Rev. Harold L. Senkbeil, executive director of Doxology and author of *Dying to Live*

"Grace is one of the most underutilized gifts Jesus has entrusted to his followers. Instead of being the air we breathe and the first thing that comes to mind when others think of us, grace, like an old fire extinguisher, gets left in the closet for occasional emergency use. *One Way Love* brings grace out in the open—showing us why we can't live without it and alerting us to its earthshaking potency to transform lives and relationships. This book left me longing to inhale God's grace more deeply, to learn more of His relentless heart of love, and to be an agent of His grace to others."

Carolyn Custis James, author of *Half the Church*

"The world desperately needs to hear about the shocking reality of God's one-way love for the undeserving—the message of grace. As is always the case with grace, those who think they are doing pretty well by underestimating their need and overestimating their ability will hate this message. But those who are desperate for grace and know they need it—the weary and heavy-laden—will find joy and relief at God's inexhaustible grace powerfully and beautifully articulated in this book. I'm immensely grateful to Tullian for his obsession with grace and for writing this potent book. I need it. You need it. We all need it."

Justin S. Holcomb, author of *On the Grace of God* and adjunct professor of theology at Reformed Theological Seminary

"The fact that the law is written on our hearts is evident in the drive within us all to justify our existence through what we do. Christians are sometimes the most driven doers of all, desperately trying to prove to God that we are worthy of the sacrifice of His son. In contrast, Tullian invites us to step off the treadmill of performancism and be truly refreshed by the height and depth of God's grace, which points us to the perfect life of Another. As a driven doer myself, I need to hear this message over and over again."

Dr. Iain Duguid, author and professor of
Old Testament at Grove City College

"Some people write about grace as if it is a new law, practically scolding us for not living by it. Tullian helps us see how utterly amazing grace is so that we discover afresh that this is precisely how we *want* to live."

Mark Galli, editor of *Christianity Today*

"Tullian Tchividjian awakens us to the fact that God doesn't offer second chances because He doesn't need to. He has already provided us with the grace to cover us in every situation, no matter where we started from, where we have been, or where we are. What a powerful message for the women I minister to who feel "stuck" and are having trouble moving their lives ahead. I recommend this book to all those who have a problem accepting themselves. *One Way Love* reminds us to get out of ourselves and accept what has already been done for us. Our lives are already treasures of the Master, who paved the way long before we were born."

Pat Smith, TV personality, speaker,
and founder of Treasure You

ONE WAY LOVE

INEXHAUSTIBLE GRACE FOR AN EXHAUSTED WORLD

TULLIAN TCHIVIDJIAN

David C Cook

transforming lives together

ONE WAY LOVE
Published by David C Cook
4050 Lee Vance View
Colorado Springs, CO 80918 U.S.A.

David C Cook Distribution Canada
55 Woodslee Avenue, Paris, Ontario, Canada N3L 3E5

David C Cook U.K., Kingsway Communications
Eastbourne, East Sussex BN23 6NT, England

The graphic circle C logo is a registered trademark of David C Cook.

LCCN 2013944266
ISBN 978-0-7814-0690-1
eISBN 978-0-7814-1089-2

© 2013 Tullian Tchividjian
Published in association with Yates & Yates, www.yates2.com.

The Team: Alex Field, Amy Konyndyk, Nick Lee, Tonya Osterhouse, Karen Athen
Cover Design: Amy Konyndyk

Printed in the United States of America
First Edition 2013

5 6 7 8 9 10

061914

To my son Nate
Your confidence, generosity, humor, tenderness,
humility, bravery, teachability, and selflessness are
a great testimony to what happens when someone
understands how God's one-way love secures them.

CONTENTS

ACKNOWLEDGMENTS

This book started out as a series of sermons I preached a couple of years ago entitled "Pictures of Grace." It was my attempt to explore the crazy, counterintuitive nature of God's grace as seen through various episodes in the life and ministry of Jesus. Convinced that grace is *way* more drastic, *way* more gratuitous, *way* more liberating, and *way* more scandalous than any of us realize, I sought to help our church get a better grip on grace, realizing that what we need most is to be startled, surprised, even shocked by it.

But this book is not the sermons. Well, it would be more accurate to say that this book is much, much more than the sermons. And for that, I have a few people I really want to thank.

My good friend Elyse Fitzpatrick took the transcriptions and provided a working draft. It's not an easy thing to go through pages and pages of transcribed sermons and "clean things up." Elyse is the best of the best. Thank you, friend!

Once Elyse was done, my good friend David Zahl and I went to work. David's skill with words, existential "in-touch-ness," and theological insightfulness is a rare combination. He filled in the gaps, provided the polish, and made this book what it is from beginning to end. As I've said before, he is a writer/editor/thinker of the highest rank. Thanks, David! You and I both know this book would not exist without you!

I also want to thank my agent, Sealy Yates, who believes in what God has compelled me to say and wants to do everything he can to help me say it.

And finally, I want to thank my Coral Ridge church family. It's a privilege to be your pastor. I'm grateful beyond words for your willingness to wrestle with the scandalous nature of God's amazing grace week in and week out.

INTRODUCTION

A few years ago, I read something astonishing. Dr. Richard Leahy, a prominent psychologist and anxiety specialist, was quoted as saying, "The average high school kid today has the same level of anxiety as the average psychiatric patient in the early 1950s."[1] It turns out the problem wasn't limited to an age group. In 2007, *The New York Times* reported that three in ten American women confess to taking sleeping pills before bed most nights.[2] The numbers are so high and unprecedented that some are calling it an epidemic.

This came across my screen about the same time that the news broke about the meteoric rise of Americans claiming no religious affiliation, shooting up from 7 percent in 1990 to 16 percent in 2010.[3] When those under the age of thirty were polled, that percentage more than doubled again, to nearly 35 percent.[4] While the numbers themselves were a bit of a shock, I wish I had been more surprised by the findings. From my vantage point as a pastor, I can tell you, it is truly heartbreaking out there. The Good News of God's inexhaustible grace for an exhausted world has never been more urgent.

What I see more than anything else is an unquestioning embrace of performancism in all sectors of life. Performancism is the mindset that equates our identity and value directly to our performance and accomplishments. Performancism casts achievement not as something we do or don't do but as something we are or aren't. The colleges those teenagers eventually attend will be more than the place where they are educated—they will be the labels that define the students' values as human beings in the eyes of their peers, their parents, and themselves. The money we earn, the cars we drive aren't merely reflective of our occupation; they are reflective of us, period. How we look, how intelligent we are, and what people think of us are more than descriptive; they are synonymous with our worth. In the world of performancism, success equals life, and failure is tantamount to death. This is the reason why people would rather end their lives than confess that they've lost their jobs or made a bad investment.

This is not to say that accomplishments are somehow bad, or even that they aren't incredibly important. It is simply to say that there is a difference between taking pride in what we do and worshipping it. When we worship at the altar of performance—and make no mistake, performancism is a form of worship—we spend our lives frantically propping up our images or reputations, trying to do it all—and do it all well—often at a cost to ourselves and those we love. Life becomes a hamster wheel of endless earning and proving and maintenance and management and controlling, where all we can see is our own feet. Performancism causes us to live in a constant state of anxiety, fear, and resentment until we end up heavily medicated, in the hospital, or just really, really unhappy.

Sadly, the Christian church has not proven to be immune to performancism. Far from it, in fact. In recent years, a handful of books have been published urging a more robust, radical, and sacrificial expression of the Christian faith. I even wrote one of them— *Unfashionable: Making a Difference in the World by Being Different*. I heartily amen the desire to take one's faith seriously and demonstrate before the watching world a willingness to be more than just Sunday churchgoers. That Christians would want to engage the wider community with God's sacrificial love—living for their neighbors instead of for themselves—is a wonderful thing and should be applauded. The unintended consequence of this push, however, is that if we're not careful, we can give people the impression that Christianity is first and foremost about the sacrifice we make for Jesus rather than the sacrifice Jesus made for us; our performance for him rather than his performance for us; our obedience for him rather than his obedience for us. The hub of Christianity is *not* "do something for Jesus." The hub of Christianity is "Jesus has done everything for you." And my fear is that too many people, both inside and outside the church, have heard our pleas for intensified devotion and concluded that the focus of Christian faith is our love for God instead of God's love for us. Don't get me wrong—what we do is important. But it is infinitely less important than what Jesus has done for us.

Furthermore, it often seems that the Good News of God's grace has been tragically hijacked by an oppressive religious moralism that is all about rules, rules, and more rules. Doing more, trying harder, self-help, getting better, and fixing, fixing, fixing—ourselves, our kids, our spouses, our friends, our enemies, our culture, our world. Christianity is perceived as being a vehicle for good behavior and clean living—and the judgments that result from them—rather than the only recourse for those who have failed over and over and over again.

Sadly, too many churches have helped to perpetuate the impression that Christianity is primarily concerned with legislating morality. Believe it or not, Christianity is not about good people getting better. If anything, it is good news for bad people coping with their failure to be good. The heart of the Christian faith is Good News, not good advice, good technique, or good behavior. Too many people have walked away from the church, not because they're walking away from Jesus, but because the church has walked away from Jesus. Ask any of the "religious nones" who answered their census questions differently in past years, and I guarantee you will hear a story about either spiritual burnout or heavy-handed condemnation from fellow believers, or both. Author Jerry Bridges puts it perfectly when he writes:

> My observation of Christendom is that most of us tend to base our relationship with God on our performance instead of on His grace. If we've performed well—whatever "well" is in our opinion—then we expect God to bless us. If we haven't done so well, our expectations are reduced accordingly. In this sense, we live by works, rather than by grace. We are saved by grace, but we are living by the "sweat" of our own performance.

Moreover, we are always challenging ourselves and one another to "try harder." We seem to believe success in the Christian life (however we define success) is basically up to us: our commitment, our discipline, and our zeal, with some help from God along the way. We give lip service to the attitude of the Apostle Paul, "But by the grace of God I am what I am (1 Cor. 15:10), but our unspoken motto is, "God helps those who help themselves."[5]

What Bridges describes is nothing less than the human compulsion for taking the reins of our lives and our salvation back from God, the only One remotely qualified for the job. *Works righteousness* is the term the Protestant Reformation used to describe spiritual performancism, and it has plagued the church—and the world—since the Garden of Eden. It might not be too much of an overstatement to say that if Jesus came to proclaim good news to the poor and release to the captives, to restore sight to the blind and give freedom for the oppressed, then Christianity has come to stand for—and in practice promulgate—the exact opposite of what its founder intended (Luke 4:18–19).

To be clear, I do not mean to imply that Christians don't believe in grace. It is just that we have a hard time with grace alone. As Max Lucado recently observed, "It wasn't that [certain Christians in the book of Acts] didn't believe in grace at all. They did. They believed in grace a lot. They just didn't believe in grace alone."[6] This book is a clarion call away from "grace a lot" and toward "grace alone." In other words, it's a passionate plea backward—back to the time when

brave men like Martin Luther staked their lives on the sola of grace.
As Robert Capon writes:

> The Reformation was a time when men went
> blind, staggering drunk because they had discov-
> ered, in the dusty basement of late medievalism, a
> whole cellar full of fifteen-hundred-year-old, two-
> hundred proof Grace—bottle after bottle of pure
> distilate of Scripture, one sip of which would con-
> vince anyone that God saves us single-handedly.
> The word of the Gospel—after all those centuries
> of trying to lift yourself into heaven by worrying
> about the perfection of your bootstraps—suddenly
> turned out to be a flat announcement that the
> saved were home before they started.[7]

It has been roughly five hundred years since the Reformation.
And looking at the church today, it is obvious that we are overdue
for another one. Indeed, what a terrible irony it is that the very
pack of people who claim that God has unconditionally saved
and continues to sustain them by His free grace are the same ones
who push back most violently against it. Far too many professing
Christians sound like ungrateful children who can't stop biting
the hand that feeds them. It amazes me that you will hear great
concern from inside the church about too much grace, but rarely
will you ever hear great concern from inside the church about
too many rules. Indeed, the absurdity of God's indiscriminate
compassion always gets "religious" people up in arms. Why?

Because we are, by nature, glory-hoarding, self-centered control freaks—God wannabes. That's why.

But the situation is more than ironic; it is tragic. It is tragic, because this kind of moralism can be relied upon to create anxiety, resentment, rebellion, and exhaustion. It can be counted upon to ensure that the church hemorrhages the precise people whom Jesus was most concerned with: sinners.

Are you exhausted? Angry? Anxious? Fearful? Guilty? Lonely? In need of some comfort and *genuinely* good news? In other words, are you at all like me? Then this book is for you. I can't promise it will answer all your questions or cover every theological base. But I can promise that you won't hear any buts, you won't feel the tapping of the brakes, and you won't read a list of qualifications. What you will encounter is "grace unmeasured, vast and free"—the kind that will frighten and free you at the same time. That's what grace does, after all.

It is high time for the church to honor its Founder by embracing *sola gratia* anew, to reignite the beacon of hope for the hopeless and point all of us bedraggled performancists back to the freedom and rest of the Cross. To leave our ifs, ands, or buts behind and get back to proclaiming the only message that matters—and the only message we *have*—the Word about God's one-way love for sinners. It is time for us to abandon, once and for all, our play-it-safe religion and get drunk on grace. Two-hundred-proof, unflinching grace. It's shocking and scary, unnatural and undomesticated, but it is also the only thing that can set us free and light the church—and the world—on fire.

CHAPTER 1

AN EXHAUSTED WORLD

If you eat your broccoli, you can have some dessert. If you clean up your room, you'll get a star, and if you get a star, then Mom and Dad will be happy. If you get good grades, you will pass the class, and if you pass the class, you will graduate. If you work hard, you'll make some money, and if you get enough money, you can buy that car. If you have a nice car, she might finally go out with you, and if you treat her nice, she may stick around. If you hurt her feelings, though, and need her forgiveness, you'll have to say you're sorry. But if she agrees to marry you, then maybe the guys at work will look at you differently, and of course, if you get their respect, you might be considered for that promotion. There will be more responsibilities, so you had better perform, because if you don't, the company won't have a good quarter, and, well, there might have to be some cutbacks.

If you lose your job, you might not be able to provide for your family, and schools aren't cheap. There are no free lunches, after all. Even broccoli is getting more expensive these days.

The fact is, real life is long on law and short on grace—the demands never stop, the failures pile up, and fears set in. Life requires many things from us—a successful career, a stable marriage, well-behaved and emotionally adjusted children, a certain quality of life. When life gets hard, the hardworking work harder. Is it any wonder we're all so tired? We do our best to do better, do more, and do now. The cultural pressure to take care of yourself and "make it happen" by working harder and smarter wears us out. We live with long lists of things to accomplish and people to please. Anyone living inside the guilt, anxiety, stress, strain, and uncertainty of daily life knows from instinct, and hard experience, that the weight of life is heavy.[1] We are all in need of some relief.

Whoever said life is a two-way street was on to something. Reward and punishment, this for that, reciprocity—whatever you want to call it—defines more than just our economy. Our relationships, our careers, our institutions also run on the principle of "I'll do X for you, if you do Y for me." Everything in our world demands two-way love. Everything's conditional. If you love me, only then will I love you. If you give to me, only then will I give to you. If you serve me, only then will I serve you. This conditionality plagues us at every turn and keeps us enslaved to fear, reservation, and insecurity. Owing and deserving seem to be written into the fabric of human nature and civilization.

Most of the time, conditionality makes our lives easier and less confusing. If we can simply find the right set of conditions to meet and then we meet them, our happiness is secured. "Give me three steps to a happy marriage, and I can guarantee myself a happy marriage … if I can simply follow the three steps." It gives us something to count on, both on a personal and global scale. Through it, we gain safety and control—whether it be in a relationship, a career, or society in general. Every hurdle we jump, every rung we climb, brings with it momentary satisfaction before reliably revealing the next one. And there's nothing wrong with that, as far as it goes. We live in a conditional world.

The problem comes, as it always does, when things fall apart. When we can't meet our end of the bargain. For every "If you do," there's an "if you don't." For every promise of reward, there is the threat of punishment—which is where anger and sadness and insecurity and fear rear their heads. If the job isn't done right, no one gets paid. And there's a long line of people waiting to give it a try if you aren't willing to. If you don't live up to his expectations, he will dump you. If you refuse to give us what we want, we will yell and scream and make your life difficult. If she doesn't say she's sorry, you will bear a grudge. If you don't exercise regularly and eat well, you will gain weight (and you will feel bad about yourself). If you can't see how much this means to me, I will resent you. Round and round and round it goes, but the underlying message is always the same: *accomplishment precedes acceptance; achievement precedes approval.*

And this is to say nothing of *can*! Like a poor shopkeeper trying to wriggle free of a mob boss, sometimes the conditions we encounter are simply impossible to meet. Have you ever met someone who has spent their entire life trying to live up to the conditions for approval and love set by a demanding parent? Oftentimes not even the death of that parent will silence the accusation. Or perhaps you've met someone who is tormented by their own internal, impossibly high standards of behavior or success or beauty; even at their peak, they are always just shy of being good enough.

We have all sorts of ways we justify our perfectionism, but none of them can change the fact that instead of gratification, or even lasting excellence, impossible conditions ultimately produce exhaustion, bitterness, and shame. Unfortunately, this truth rarely stops us from hoisting such conditions on others and ourselves. It may be all we know.

ENTER THE CHRISTIAN FAITH

There are many things for which Christianity is known in the modern world—not all of them good. In fact, the Christian faith has often been perceived (and experienced) as the *ultimate* vehicle of conditionality. Christians may talk about God being loving and forgiving, but what they mean is that God loves and forgives those who are good and clean—who meet His conditions, in other words.

Or maybe it is more subtle than that. Maybe you are a Christian, and you rightly believe that God forgave your past indiscretions—that was what drew you to Him in the first place. But once you made that initial Christian commitment, it was time to get your act together and be serious. We conclude that it was God's blood, sweat, and tears that got us in, but that it's our blood, sweat, and tears that keep us in. We view God as a glorified bookkeeper, tallying our failures and successes on His cosmic ledger. We conclude that in order for God to love us, we have to change, grow, and be good.

Staying on the straight and narrow out of fear is incredibly stressful, but you tell yourself it's better than the alternative: naked trust in the too-good-to-be-true goodness of Someone you can't control. There is, after all, no free lunch. If you want love, you must earn it.

I exaggerate, but not much. Hence the scores of "sad and mad alumnae of the Christian faith."[2] Yet the tragic irony is that, contrary to popular assumptions, the Bible is a not a record of the blessed good, but rather the blessed bad. That's not a typo. *The Bible is a record of the blessed bad.* The Bible is not a witness to the best people making it up to God; it's a witness to God making it down to the worst people. Far from being a book full of moral heroes whom we are commanded to emulate, what we discover is that the so-called heroes in the Bible are not really heroes at all. They fall and fail; they make huge mistakes; they get afraid; they're selfish, deceptive, egotistical, and unreliable. The Bible is one long story of God meeting our rebellion with His rescue, our sin with His salvation, our guilt with His grace, our badness with His goodness. The overwhelming focus of the Bible is not the work of the redeemed but the work of the Redeemer. Which means that the Bible is not first a recipe book for Christian living but a revelation book of Jesus who is the answer to our un-Christian living.

This sad misperception is something I sincerely hope might be dispelled in this book. But let's not limit the scope of the issue: the oppressiveness of conditionality is a human reality, not an exclusively Christian one. The wider world is chock-full of ladders to climb and clubs to join, two-way streets where the traffic often seems to be going in reverse. Everyone knows what it is like not to measure up in some arena.

Fortunately, no amount of bad press, whether deserved or undeserved, has been able to fully obscure the core message of Christianity—its most urgent contribution and the basis of its captivating power—which has to do with the beauty and freedom of God's unconditional love. This book seeks to recover and reiterate that word of tremendous hope in an honest and accessible way for the sake of those suffering under the weight of conditionality, which is everyone. It is concerned with the miraculous Good News of God's inexhaustible grace for an exhausted world.

GRACE, GRACE, AND MORE GRACE

What is grace? The definition for this book comes from Paul Zahl. He writes:

> Grace is love that seeks you out when you have nothing to give in return. Grace is love coming at you that has nothing to do with you. Grace is being loved when you are unlovable…. The cliché definition of grace is "unconditional love." It is a true cliché, for it is a good description of the thing….
>
> Let's go a little further, though. Grace is a love that has nothing to do with you, the beloved. It has everything and only to do with the lover. Grace is irrational in the sense that it has nothing to do with weights and measures. It has nothing to do with my intrinsic qualities or so-called "gifts" (whatever

they may be). It reflects a decision on the part of the
giver, the one who loves, in relation to the receiver,
the one who is loved, that negates any qualifications
the receiver may personally hold…. Grace is *one-
way love*.[3]

Grace doesn't make demands. It just gives. And from our vantage point, it always gives to the wrong person. We see this over
and over again in the Gospels: Jesus is always giving to the wrong
people—prostitutes, tax collectors, half-breeds. The most extravagant sinners of Jesus's day receive his most compassionate welcome.
Grace is a divine vulgarity that stands caution on its head. It refuses
to play it safe and lay it up. Grace is recklessly generous, uncom-
fortably promiscuous. It doesn't use sticks, carrots, or time cards. It
doesn't keep score. As Robert Capon puts it, "Grace works without
requiring *anything* on our part. It's not expensive. It's not even cheap.
It's free."[4] It refuses to be controlled by our innate sense of fairness,
reciprocity, and evenhandedness. It defies logic. It has nothing to do
with earning, merit, or deservedness. It is opposed to what is owed. It
doesn't expect a return on investments. It is a liberating contradiction
between what we deserve and what we get. Grace is unconditional
acceptance given to an undeserving person by an unobligated giver.
It is one-way love.

Think about it in your own life for a moment. Odds are you
have caught a glimpse of one-way love at some point, and it made all
the difference. Someone let you off the hook when you least expected
or deserved it. A friend suspended judgment at a key moment. Your
father was lenient when you wrecked his car. Your teacher gave you an

extension, even though she knew you had been procrastinating. You said something insensitive to your spouse, and instead of retaliating, she kept quiet and somehow didn't hold it against you the next day. If you're married, odds are the person you ended up with showed you this kind of love at some point along the line.

One-way love is rare, though, and it always comes as a surprise. Fortunately, the glimpses we receive in relationships are only a foreshadowing of God's love for us. They are like little arrows that point to the very heart of the universe, what Dante called "the Love that moves the Sun and the other stars," the love that received its fullest expression in the person and work of Jesus Christ. When John writes that "God is love," he is talking about Jesus (1 John 4:8–9). Indeed, if we're to explore this subject in any depth, there's no better backdrop than Jesus's life and teaching. Each chapter will look at a different episode from his ministry.

When the chain of quid pro quo is broken, all sorts of wonderful things can happen. One-way love has the unique power to inspire generosity, kindness, loyalty, and more love, precisely because it removes any and all requirement to change or produce. As some of the stories in later chapters will attest, it is the only thing that has had that power in my own life. It has been the difference between joy and sadness, gratitude and entitlement, life and death. In fact, the older I get, the more I realize how much my life is one long testament to this abiding truth. I'm not overstating things when I say that discovering the message of God's one-way love in all its radical glory has saved my marriage, my relationship with my kids, and my ministry. So this is not an abstract subject to me. One-way love is my lifeblood.

And yet, as beautiful and lifesaving as grace can be, we often resist it. By nature, we are suspicious of promises that seem too good to be true. We wonder about the ulterior motives of the excessively generous. We long ago stopped opening those emails and letters that tell us what we've "already won." *What's the catch? What's the fine print? What's in it for them?*

Grace is a gift, pure and simple. We might insist on trying to pay, but the balance has been settled (and our money's no good!). Of course, even if we're able to accept one-way love when it comes *our* way, we have trouble when it reaches other people, especially those who've done us wrong. As we will explore in subsequent chapters, grace offends our sense of justice by being both implausible and unfair.

We are uncomfortable because grace turns the tables on us, relieving us of our precious sense of control. It tears up the time card we were counting on to be assured of that nice, big paycheck on Friday. It forces us to rely on the goodness of Another, and that, dear friends, is simply terrifying. However much we may hate having to get up and go to the salt mines every day, we distrust the thought of completely resting in the promised generosity of God even more. So we try to domesticate the message of one-way love—after all, who could trust in or believe something so radically unbelievable? Robert Capon articulates the prayer of the grace-averse heart:

> Restore to us, Preacher, the comfort of merit and
> demerit. Prove for us that there is at least something
> we can do, that we are still, at whatever dim recess
> of our nature, the masters of our relationships. Tell

us, Prophet, that in spite of all our nights of losing,
there will yet be one redeeming card of our very
own to fill the inside straight we have so long and
so earnestly tried to draw to. But whatever you do,
do not preach grace… We insist on being reckoned
with. Give us something, anything; but spare us the
indignity of this indiscriminate acceptance.[5]

The idea that there is an unconditional love that relieves the
pressure, forgives our failures, and replaces our fear with faith seems
too good to be true. Longing for hope in a world of hype, the Gospel
of Jesus Christ is the news we have been waiting for all our lives:
God loves real people like you and me, which He demonstrated by
sending His real Son to set real people free.

Jesus came to liberate us from the weight of having to make it
on our own, from the demand to measure up. He came to emanci-
pate us from the burden to get it all right, from the obligation to fix
ourselves, find ourselves, and free ourselves. Jesus came to release us
from the slavish need to be right, rewarded, regarded, and respected.
Because Jesus came to set the captives free, life does not have to be
a tireless effort to establish ourselves, justify ourselves, and validate
ourselves.

The Gospel of Jesus Christ announces that because Jesus was
strong for you, you're free to be weak. Because Jesus won for you,
you're free to lose. Because Jesus was Someone, you're free to be
no one. Because Jesus was extraordinary, you're free to be ordinary.
Because Jesus succeeded for you, you're free to fail. One way to sum-
marize God's message to the worn out and weary is like this—God's

demand: "be righteous"; God's diagnosis: "no one is righteous"; God's deliverance: "Jesus is our righteousness." Once this good news grips your heart, it changes everything. It frees you from having to be perfect. It frees you from having to hold it all together. In the place of exhaustion, you might even find energy.

No, the Gospel of grace is *not* too good to be true. It is true! It's the truest truth in the entire universe. God loves us independently of what we may or may not bring to the table. There are no strings attached! No ifs, ands, or buts. No qualifiers or conditions. No need for balance. No broccoli in sight! Grace is the most dangerous, expectation-wrecking, smile-creating, counterintuitive reality there is.

Grace is a bit like a roller coaster; it makes us scream in terror and laugh uncontrollably at the same time. But there aren't any harnesses on this ride. We are not in the driver's seat, and we did not design the twists and turns. We just get on board. We laugh as the binding law of gravity is suspended, and we scream because it looks like we're going to hurtle off into space. Grace brings us back into contact with the children we once were (and still are)—children who loved to ride roller coasters, to smile and yell and throw our hands up in the air. Grace, in other words, is terrifyingly fun, and like any ride worth standing in line for, it is worth coming back to again and again. In fact, God's one-way love may be the only ride that never gets old, the only ride we thankfully never outgrow. A source of inexhaustible hope and joy for an exhausted world.

So what are we waiting for? Scoot over, and let's take the plunge, once again, for the first time.

CHAPTER 2

HOW I ALMOST KILLED MY MOTHER

I was sixteen when my parents kicked me out of the house. What started out as run-of-the-mill adolescent rebellion in my early teens had, over the course of a few short years, blossomed into a black hole of disrespect and self-centeredness that was consuming the entire family. I would lie when I didn't have to, push every envelope, pick fights with my siblings, carry on, and sneak around—at first in innocent ways; later in not-so-innocent ways. If someone said "black," I would say "white." Nothing all that terrible by the world's standards, but given my Christian context and upbringing, it was pretty egregious. Eventually, everyone involved reached the end of their patience, and looking back, I can't blame them. It's not as though my parents hadn't tried every other option. Private school, public school, homeschool, counseling, interventions—you name it.

Anything they did just made me want to rebel more. Eventually, my lifestyle became so disruptive, the fights so brutal, that my parents were forced to say, "We love you, son, but if you're going to continue living this way, you can't do so under our roof."

After they kicked me out, I dropped out of high school. I thought it was the best thing that had ever happened to me, and it may have been—but not for the reasons I surmised. Those first two years, I floated from one friend's house to another's, doing odd jobs, just barely making ends meet, pursuing freedom with every ounce of my being, somehow convinced that without parents and teachers looking over my shoulder, all my problems would be solved. They weren't. The opposite, in fact. When I turned eighteen, I was finally able to get an apartment of my own, which turned up the volume considerably on my South Florida–style debauchery. I would get a job, do something stupid, get fired. My parents would bail me out, and then I'd go out and do it again. I put them through hell! I wasn't happy, not at all, but I did learn quite a bit about myself, my family, and, ultimately, about God. In fact, it was the beginning of my personal crash course in one-way love.

A TALE OF TWO SONS

The Bible is positively saturated with the message of one-way love, a number of instances of which I will be unpacking in these pages. We'll read in bewilderment as Christ comforts a broken-down prostitute. We'll see him excoriate those oh-so-punctilious keepers of the salt mines, the Pharisees, who would bar the weak, weary, and wounded from their personal spiritual bank account.

We'll hear him speak his Father's words of mercy as he answers the humble whispers of a traitorous loan shark. We'll squirm as he probes our sense of right and wrong, our love of conditionality, with questions like, "Do you resent my generosity?" Then we'll see him purposely subvert the rules so that we might learn that mercy trumps them all. In fact, before we continue, let's take a step back and look at what may be the most famous picture of one-way love in the Bible—the parable that hits extremely close to home for me, the parable of the two sons, traditionally called the parable of the prodigal son.

> And [Jesus] said, "There was a man who had two sons. And the younger of them said to his father, 'Father, give me the share of property that is coming to me.' And he divided his property between them. Not many days later, the younger son gathered all he had and took a journey into a far country, and there he squandered his property in reckless living. And when he had spent everything, a severe famine arose in that country, and he began to be in need. So he went and hired himself out to one of the citizens of that country, who sent him into his fields to feed pigs. And he was longing to be fed with the pods that the pigs ate, and no one gave him anything. But when he came to himself, he said, 'How many of my father's hired servants have more than enough bread, but I perish here with hunger!'"
> (Luke 15:11–17)

The prodigal son may have left his home voluntarily, but I'm not so sure he and I are all that different. I made it very clear to everyone around me that I couldn't wait to get out on my own and live the life. The prodigal son is more direct. He goes to his father and says, "I want my share of the inheritance right now." In those days, a son did not get his share of the inheritance until his father died, so he was essentially saying, "Dad, as far as I'm concerned, you're dead to me, and since you won't oblige and kick off, just give me my share of the inheritance now." Unloving, entitled, disrespectful, and rude. Sound familiar?

I know what my dad would have said, and as a father, I know what I would say if one of my sons asked me to give him his inheritance. This father knows how reckless and self-destructive his son is being, and he knows his son is going to squander whatever he gives him. So what does he do? He turns everything we think we know about raising responsible children on its head and gives the boy what he asks. We read that and think, *What an unwise father. If this father had been steeped in the proverbial wisdom of the Bible, he would have never made such a foolish mistake.* But the father knows something we don't. He knows that in order to win the heart of his son, he has to risk losing him altogether by giving him something even more dangerous and reckless than what he asked for. He has to give him grace.

Sure enough, the son goes out and blows his inheritance on women and wine. When he finally wakes up and finds himself in a pigsty, he takes the only option left to him—namely, to get up and sheepishly return to his father. On the way back home, he rehearses his speech:

Father, I have sinned against heaven and before you.
I am no longer worthy to be called your son. Treat
me as one of your hired servants. (Luke 15:18–19)

Of course, his father has been waiting for this moment, and when, from a distance, he sees the bedraggled boy coming, he feels such great compassion and love that he runs out and embraces his son. Then, in a radically undignified manner, the father falls in the dirt and hugs his child's legs. The son launches into his groveling speech, but before he can get the lines out, the father clothes him in the best robe and puts a ring on his finger and shoes on his feet. He restores his lost son's status before the son even has the chance to say or do *anything*. The son brings nothing to the table; it is a one-way transaction. Why? Because the father already has one son who thinks he's a hired servant. He doesn't need another.

Note that the father never once says, "I will welcome you back only if you detail for me all the mistakes you have made, so I can determine whether you're truly sorry and ready to be part of the family again." Think of that! The father doesn't demand anything from this son, who has put him through so much pain. He does not insist on emotional, financial, or legal consequences. He doesn't drag the boy into court or make him stand up in front of the local religious leaders and do penance. Instead he rewards him. He gives him the very opposite of what he deserves. The father knows that his son is already acutely aware of his guilt and shame—the boy knows what he has done—what he needs is to be forgiven.

Brennan Manning, an author who knew a whole lot more about one-way love than I ever will, summed it up this way:

My message, unchanged for more than fifty years, is this: *God loves you unconditionally, as you are and not as you should be, because nobody is as they should be.* It is the message of grace.... A grace that pays the eager beaver who works all day long the same wages as the grinning drunk who shows up at ten till five. A grace that hikes up the robe and runs breakneck toward the prodigal reeking of sin and wraps him up and decides to throw a party no *ifs*, *ands*, or *buts*....

This vulgar grace is indiscriminate compassion. It works without asking anything of us.... Grace is sufficient even though we huff and puff with all our might to try to find something or someone it cannot cover. Grace is enough.... Jesus is enough.[1]

Needless to say, in our everyday lives, bad behavior and poor performance are rarely met with this kind of response. Punishment and reproach are much more common—and reasonable. People need to be held accountable for their actions! There must be consequences! "We are not doormats," we tell ourselves. The truth is, we are much more comfortable with conditionality, with two-way relationships in which we love those who treat us well and punish those who hurt us, than we are with anything resembling unconditional love. Regardless of how much we may want others to be merciful with us, when the tables are turned, we find it virtually impossible not to judge. Yet we also know that those times when we've caught glimpses of grace have been transformative—maybe not immediately, but eventually. During those rocky teenage years I experienced both.

A TALE OF TWO LUNCHES

My parents were well loved in our community, and their friends could see the heartache they were going through with me. I remember two separate instances of people caring enough to ask them for permission to talk with me one-on-one to see if maybe they could get through to me. The first time was early on, when I was still living at home. Their friend picked me up after school, brought me to Burger King, and read me the riot act.

"Look at all that God's given you. You're squandering everything. You're making your parents' life a living hell, acting so selfishly, not considering your siblings. You go to a private school. You have this remarkable heritage. Shape up, man! Snap out of it."

Of course, he was 100 percent right. In fact, if he had known the full truth of what I was up to (and what was in my heart), he would have had every reason to be even harsher. But in the first five minutes of this guy talking to me, I could tell where it was going, and I just tuned out. As far as I was concerned, it was white noise. I could not wait for it to be over and for him to drop me back off at home.

This first friend was the voice of the law. He was articulating the standard that I was falling short of—what I should have been doing and who I should have been being—and he couldn't have been more correct. The condemnation was entirely justified. His words gave an accurate description of who I was at that moment. But that's the curious thing about the law and judgment in general: it can tell us who we are, it can tell us the right thing to do, but it cannot inspire us to do that thing or be that person. In fact, it often creates the opposite reaction than the one that is intended. It certainly did for me! I don't blame the man in question—he was trying to do the right thing. It's just that his methods completely backfired.

The second experience happened about a year and a half later, and by this time I was out of the house. This man called me and said, "I'd love to meet with you."

And I thought, *Oh no, another one of my parents' friends trying to set me straight.* But I didn't want to make things any worse between my parents and me, and the free meal didn't sound too bad either, so I agreed to get together with him.

Once we were at the restaurant, he just looked at me and said, "Listen, I know you're going through a tough time, and I know life must seem very confusing right now. And I just want to tell you that I love you, I'm here for you, and I think God's going to do great things with you. Here's my phone number. If you ever need anything, call me. If you want to tell me something you don't feel comfortable telling anybody else, call me. I just want you to know that I'm here for you." And then he switched the subject and started talking about sports. That guy—the second guy—is still a friend of mine to this day. He will forever be marked in my personal history as an example of amazing grace.

Even though it took place almost twenty-five years ago, I still think about our conversation all the time. I think about it because in so many ways, I'm still that kid. I haven't graduated from my need for grace, and I never will. I still want what I want when I want it, and while it may not happen quite as often, thank God, I still hurt the people I love. I wake up to the same demands that you do. I live with the same anxieties and insecurities. I know from personal experience, as you do, that the weight of life can be crushing. And even though I spend hours every day thinking and talking about grace, I struggle to believe too. But it is inside the pressing context of everyday life that one-way love becomes more than a theory, more than an idea, more than something that churchy people talk about on Sunday. It is there that one-way love becomes that which breathes life and relief into our weary, scared bones.

CONTROL FREAKS OF THE WORLD UNITE!

There is a reason why the story of the prodigal son has held people's attention over the centuries more than any other parable. Yes, it is a beautiful picture of God's one-way love, but it is more than that: it is a beautiful picture of God's one-way love for an unloving and actively hostile person. The parable is grounded, in other words, in the reality of the human condition. It does not flatter the listener. It paints us as entitled brats who disrespect our fathers and pursue our selfish ends at a cost to both ourselves and those who love us. But remember, the Gospel only sounds good to a heart that knows it is bad. For people who think they're good, grace is frustrating. For people who know they're not, grace is freeing. I know *bad* is a loaded word, so let me explain.

The Bible has a lot to say about human nature. It talks about men and women being made in the image of God, that we are fearfully and wonderfully made (Ps. 139:14), capable of great acts of love and charity. And this is true, without a doubt. Each and every day I am blown away by the amazing and sacrificial work being done both in my immediate vicinity and abroad. I thank God for it!

But the Bible also talks about our fall from grace and posits the unpopular doctrine of original sin, the notion that no one is righteous, that no part of us is free from selfishness and sin, and that the condition is sadly hereditary (Rom. 3). The great American theologian Reinhold Niebuhr once referred to original sin as "the only empirically verifiable doctrine of the Christian faith,"[2] and what he meant is simply that our histories, both global and personal, bear out the Bible's claim that our basic nature is fatally compromised. I'm afraid to say this applies just as much to Christians as it does to non-Christians. In fact, in my conversations with the believers I most admire, the ones I consider to be almost saintly, humility is always the thing that most stands out. And by humility, I mean the sense that, as they have grown older, their understanding of their need for God's grace and forgiveness has deepened rather than abated. Sin, it would seem, is comprehensive. There is no part of us that it does not touch. Our minds are affected by it. Our hearts are affected by it. Our wills are affected by it. Our bodies as well. This is at the heart of Paul's internal struggle that he articulates in Romans 7, when he says, "For I do not do the good I want, but the evil I do not want is what I keep on doing" (v. 19). If you can relate to that sentence, then this book is for you.

Even the briefest glance at a newspaper confirms this claim. We are not good people getting better, but flawed men and women who, at worst, seem to be stuck in a cycle of heartbreak and self-destruction and, at best, are learning to live with some pretty serious limitations. We are, without a doubt, broken people living with other broken people in a broken world.

This does not mean that there aren't plenty of bright spots in our lives and in our world. It simply means that as much as we might wish it were not so, our weaknesses tend to define us more than our strengths. We live where our problems are; they are the first things we think about when we wake up in the morning and the last things we worry about before we go to sleep. To know someone is to know them at their least flattering, not their shiniest.

Now you may not think of yourself as someone who is particularly rebellious or self-seeking. "I pay my taxes and read my Bible," you might say. Perhaps you read my story at the beginning of this chapter with disbelief and maybe a little disdain. "How could he?" In the parable of the prodigal son, you probably identify more with the elder brother. Yet as we will explore later, the elder brother was just as much at odds with his father as the younger one.

Rebellion and conformity are often flip sides of the same coin. To be sure, sin takes all different forms—some of them overt, some more covert, some more damaging than others (in the short term)—but none of them benign. Once we understand that sin has more to do with what's on the inside of us than what we do on the outside, we begin to see our own desperate need for grace, whether it takes the form of trying to find freedom and fullness of life by breaking the rules (younger brother) or keeping them (elder brother). The problem is that we are so accustomed to thinking about sin exclusively in terms of external behavior and outward rebellion.

DOING THE RIGHT THING FOR THE WRONG REASONS

Ethical behaviorism is a term psychologists use to describe a schema where a person's righteousness is defined exclusively in terms of what they do or do not do. In this sense, a righteous person is one who does the right things and avoids the wrong things. An unrighteous person is one who does the wrong things and avoids the right things. Defined this way, righteousness is a quality that can be judged by an observation of someone's behavior. Virtue and uprightness is purely a matter of outer conduct without any hint of what goes on inside you.

William Hordern illustrates how this definition of righteousness is the definition our culture at large has adopted:

> The law enforcement institutions of society are concerned with right behavior. They do not care why people obey the law, so long as they obey it. The person who breaks no laws is righteous in their sight regardless of the motivation that produces law-abiding behavior.[3]

In Jesus's Sermon on the Mount, he radically amplifies this definition of righteousness. He insists that righteousness is not simply a matter of what we do or don't do but rather a question of why we do or don't do it. His view of righteousness goes deeper than behavior and outward action. It always looks into a person, at the motivation of the act.

A few years ago, when my boys were younger, they would gather all the neighborhood kids in our yard to play football. And every once in a while, a pass would be overthrown, landing in my neighbor's grass. My neighbor (an angry, grumpy old curmudgeon) would always come outside and scream at my boys and their friends, threatening to confiscate the ball if it happened again. My boys, being young at the time, would always come inside with tears in their eyes, lips quivering, because they were scared of our neighbor. Being the scrapper I am, there were countless times when I wanted to march over to my neighbor and give him a piece of my mind. I wanted to make it clear that if he ever yelled at my boys again … Well, you get the idea. I never did, though. I would stare him down from time to time, but I never went next door to let him have it. Some would assume that my refusal to let loose on my neighbor was an act of righteousness: I was exercising love, patience, and self-control. But was it?

Only God and I (and now you!) know the real reason I never went off on my mean neighbor: the potential risk to me was too high. I didn't want to get in trouble. I didn't want him calling the police. I didn't want him filing a complaint against me to our neighborhood association. I didn't want him gossiping about me and causing people in the neighborhood to think less of me. After all, everyone knows I'm a pastor, and I didn't want to tarnish my image. And on and on and on. In other words, the very thing that may have, on the surface, seemed righteous was motivated by something terribly unrighteous: selfishness.

So the apparent "righteousness" of my deed was destroyed by the motivation that inspired it. It wasn't as "righteous" as it seemed, to say the least. Hordern goes on, spelling this out very clearly:

Before an act of murder or adultery is committed there has first been the motivations of the person involved. In his or her heart there has been a murderous anger or an adulterous lust. What Jesus says in the Sermon on the Mount is that many people may have the same motivations in their hearts without ever carrying out the external actions. There may be many reasons for not acting upon our motivations, but obviously one of the most common reasons is a fear of the consequences. The laws of all societies make it perilous to commit murder and laws or social pressures of all societies make it costly to commit adultery. Therefore when a person refrains from such actions it may not be because their heart is pure but simply a matter of self-protection. Jesus is saying that where the motivation for not acting on one's desire is selfish, that person is as unrighteous in God's eyes as the person who actually commits the crime.[4]

The reason this is so important is because many people inside the church think God cares only that we obey. In fact, many believe that it is even more honorable—and therefore more righteous—when we obey God against all desire to obey Him. Where did we get the idea that if we do what God tells us to do, even though "our hearts are far from Him," it's something to be proud of, something admirable, something praiseworthy, something righteous? Don't get me wrong, we *should* obey when we don't feel like it (I expect my children, for instance, to clean their rooms and respect their mother and me even when they don't feel like it). But let's not make the common mistake of proudly equating that with the righteousness that God requires.

The truth is that doing the right thing with the wrong motivation reveals deep unrighteousness, not devout righteousness. T. S. Eliot said it best:

> The last temptation is the greatest treason:
> To do the right deed for the wrong reason.[5]

If any kind of obedience, regardless of what motivates it, is what God is after, He would have showcased the Pharisees and exhorted all of us to follow their lead, to imitate them. But He didn't. Jesus called them "whitewashed tombs"—clean on the outside, dead on the inside. They had been successful in achieving behavioristic righteousness and thought that's what made them clean. But Jesus said, "So you also outwardly appear righteous to others, but within you are full of hypocrisy and lawlessness" (Matt. 23:28).

A large part of Jesus's goal in the Sermon on the Mount, particularly in Matthew 5:17–48, is to make it painfully clear that whatever we think our greatest vice is, it is actually much worse: if we think it's anger, Jesus claims it is actually murder; if we think it's lust, Jesus shows us that it is actually adultery; if we think it's impatience, Jesus says idolatry. By equating action with motivation, he kicks the legs out from under our carefully orchestrated self-salvation projects, painfully revealing our righteousness for the house of cards that it really is. His words leave no doubt that we are in need of a righteousness we can never attain on our own, an impossible righteousness that is always out of our reach. The purpose of the Sermon on the Mount is to demolish all notions that we can attain the righteousness required by God on our own.

External righteousness is something we believe we can achieve on our own with a little self-discipline (and a lot of self-righteousness). But Jesus wants us to see that regardless of how well we think we are doing or how righteous we think we're becoming, when "You therefore must be perfect, as your heavenly Father is perfect" becomes the standard and not "how much I've improved over the years," we realize that we are much further gone than we imagined ourselves to be—that our unrighteousness is inescapable, that even the best things we do have something in them that needs to be forgiven.

This is not an easy message to accept. After all, it is much harder to defend our motivations, which we can rarely dictate or fully define, than our actions, over which we have a modicum of control (most of the time!). Which is ironic, since our motivations—both our fears *and* our hopes—are universally bound up with our desire to be in control of our lives. "Give me my inheritance now. I want to be on my own, thank you very much. Now leave me alone." We want, in essence, to be our own Gods. In fact, the definition of human nature—of original sin—that I'd like to use in this book is simply that we are all people who are addicted to control (remember the serpent's words to Adam and Eve in Genesis 3: "You will be like God"). The sad irony of our lives is that our desire to be in control almost always ends up controlling us.

In his book *Grace in Addiction*, John Z. describes our situation as that of actors who think they are directors:

Can you imagine the chaos that would break out on set if one of the actors tried suddenly to usurp the director's job? The chaos probably wouldn't last very long, because the actor would soon be on his way out the door and in search of a new job!

… Imagine further the insanity that would ensue if *all* of the actors in a show somehow got the same wrong idea about their roles, and they *all* started trying to control the production simultaneously, each with a different idea of how the story should be written.[6]

This may not be an optimistic or happy picture, but it is one that accounts for much of the pain and worry that marks our lives. This rather sober view of human nature means that the great question of life is not *if* our addiction to control will cause us to act in foolish and self-seeking ways, but what will happen *when* it does. It means that the great theme of human existence is the presence or lack of love we experience in those times of defeat. It's when we come to the end of ourselves that we come to the beginning of grace.

Fortunately, and not coincidentally, the Bible is centrally occupied with these very subjects as well. *God* is centrally occupied with them. How does the Director relate to all these actors who are compulsively trying to do His job for Him (and producing disastrous results)? Does He fire them? Or does He save them?

The great hope we find in the Christian faith is that God is not us. In fact, the cross tells us that His response to people addicted to their own control is like that of the father in the parable. No matter how many times we've blown it, no matter how many years we've been unsuccessfully trying to get better, God attaches no strings to His love. None. His love for us does not depend on our loveliness. It goes one way. As far as our sin may extend, the grace of our Father extends further.

WRITING CHECKS YOU CAN(NOT) CASH

One final story to illustrate before we move on. A couple of years after I was kicked out of my home, when I was living in an apartment with some friends, I called my dad (after losing yet another of my many dead-end jobs—I called him only when I needed something) and said, "Rent's due, and I don't have any money."

My dad asked, "Well, what happened to your job?" I made up some lie about cutbacks or something. He said, "Meet me at Denny's in an hour." I said okay.

After we sat down, he signed a blank check, handed it to me, and said, "Take whatever you need. This should hold you over until you can find another job." He didn't probe into why I lost my job or yell at me for doing so. He didn't give a limit ("Here's $1,000"). And I absolutely took advantage! I not only remember taking that check and writing it out for much more than I needed, I remember sneaking into my mom and dad's house on numerous occasions and stealing checks from out of his checkbook. I mastered forging his signature. I went six months at one point without a job, because I didn't need one! Any time I needed money, I would go steal another check and forge his signature—five hundred dollars, three hundred dollars, seven hundred dollars. I completely abused his kindness—and he knew it! Years later he told me that he saw all those checks being cashed, but he decided not to say anything about it at the time. It didn't happen immediately (the fruits of grace are always in the future), but that demonstration of unconditional grace was the beginning of God doing a miraculous work in my heart and life.

Don't get me wrong. I'm not saying this is *the* pattern every time for every child in every situation. What I've given is a snapshot of one thing my father did at a very particular time for a very particular reason. As I described above, my dad handled me differently in a variety of situations. For example, my parents literally tried everything from private school to public school to homeschool to counseling, before they eventually kicked me out.

But on this occasion, at this time in my life—knowing me the way only a father can know his son—my dad did something I'm sure was scary for him, and God used it.

My father died in 2010, twenty-one years after he sent his disrespectful, ungrateful son on his way. And it was his unconditional, reckless, one-way love for me at my most arrogant and worst that God used to eventually bring me back. Until the day he died, my father was my biggest cheerleader and my best friend. I miss him every day.

Steve Brown once told me something I will never forget. He said, "Children will run from law, and they'll run from grace. The ones who run from law never come back. But the ones who run from grace always come back. Grace draws its own back home."

I ran from grace. It drew me home.

CHAPTER 3

CONFESSIONS OF A PERFORMANCIST

Legendary college football coach Urban Meyer tells a remarkable story about his father. During his senior year of high school, Urban was drafted by the Atlanta Braves to play major league baseball. Soon after arriving in the minor leagues, however, he realized he didn't have the necessary talent and called his father to tell him he was quitting. His father informed Urban that if he quit, he would no longer be welcome in their home. "Just call your mom on Christmas," he said. Needless to say, Urban finished out the season and ended up embracing the incredibly conditional world of his father, a world in which failure was simply not an option and *reflection* another word for "weakness wrapped in nostalgia."

Urban went on to win back-to-back national championships as the coach for the Florida Gators, and some would chalk his success up to his uncompromising attitude and work ethic. It certainly helped. But it turns out that these victories were short-lived, at least as far as Urban was concerned. The screws only got tighter; once he had won those titles, anything but perfection would be viewed as failure. After the 2007 season, Urban apparently confessed to a friend that anxiety was taking over his life and he wanted to walk away. He was quoted in 2011 as saying, "Building takes passion and energy. Maintenance is awful. It's nothing but fatigue. Once you reach the top, maintaining that beast is awful."[1] In that same interview, the reporter described him as a "man who destroys himself running for a finish line that doesn't exist." Soon the chest pains started, and then they started getting worse. A few hours after the Gators' winning streak finally came to an end in 2009, Urban was found on the floor of his house, unable to move or speak. He had come to a breaking point. Soon he would resign, come back, and resign again.

Urban Meyer's story may be a bit extreme, but perhaps you can relate. Perhaps you had a demanding father or mother, for whom nothing was ever good enough. Perhaps they are long gone, but you still hear their voice in your head. Perhaps you have a spouse who never seems to let up with the demands, for whom successes are not really successes; they're simply nonfailures. You see, as gifted and driven as Urban Meyer was and is, no one can live under the burden of perfection forever. It may work for a while, but sooner or later, we hit the wall. Even when Urban was fulfilling all righteousness record-wise, he wasn't doing it out of love of the game or the joy of shepherding young men, but out of fear of weakness and fear of what it would mean if he lost. If righteousness is a matter of motivation as well as action, as we talked about in the last chapter, then even when he was meeting the standards of performance set by his father, he wasn't really meeting them.

Urban had fallen victim to a vicious form of performancism. He had become a slave to his record, where the points scored on the field were more than just a proud part of his team's tally but a measure of his personal worth and identity.

I got my first tennis racket on my seventh birthday. And because we had a tennis court in our backyard, I played every day. By ten I was playing competitively. Everyone around me marveled at my natural ability. I would constantly hear how great I was for being so young, how much potential I had to "really go somewhere." All of this made me feel important. It made me feel like I mattered. Without realizing it, I began to anchor my sense of worth and value in being a great tennis player.

I had a problem, though. Whenever I would hit a bad shot or lose a point, I would throw a John McEnroe–like temper tantrum. I would yell, curse, break my racket, etc. Numerous times, my parents and coaches would counsel me, telling me I had to get myself under control. But I couldn't. No matter how hard I tried, I just couldn't. I didn't know why back then, but I do now. Every lost point, game, set, and match threatened my identity. I unconsciously concluded that if I didn't become the best, I'd be a nobody. If I didn't win, I didn't count. If I wasn't successful, I would be worthless.

I was experiencing what one of my favorite teachers calls "the law of capability"—the law that judges us wanting if we're not capable, if we can't handle it all, if we don't meet the expectations we put on ourselves or others put on us:

If I can do enough of the right things, I will have established my value. Identity is the sum of my achievements. Hence, if I can satisfy the boss, meet the needs of my spouse and children, and still pursue my dreams, then I will be somebody. In Christian theology, such a position is called justification by works. It assumes that my worth is measured by my performance. Conversely, it conceals a dark and ghastly fear: If I do not perform, I will be judged unworthy. To myself I will cease to exist.[2]

IT'S A LEGAL MATTER, BABY

Before we can really talk about one-way love, we need to understand its inverse: two-way love (which isn't really love at all). Performancism is, after all, essentially a two-way street. Conditionality, through and through: If you perform well, then you are a person of value. If you don't, then you aren't. If you stick with the team, you can still call yourself my son. You do your part, and you'll get what you deserve. Performancism speaks the language of earning, rather than the language of giving. It is a secular expression of what the Bible calls the Law.

Law, of course, is a word with which we are all familiar. It refers to the code of rules and regulations that govern our society, outlining what is permissible and what isn't. Our conduct, both individual and corporate, is judged according to it. The Law of God is similar but more comprehensive. It dictates more than just proper behavior; it dictates morality itself. In it, we find the definition of what is right and wrong, good and bad, what "thou shalt" and "thou shalt not." One way to think of the Law of God would be as the divine "Ought." It goes without saying that the author of the Law is God Himself—not us—and as such, the Law is good and perfect and true. I'll say it again: the Law is good!

A few important notes on the nature of the Law before we continue. First, the Law carries an imperative. The most famous iteration of the Law in the Bible is the Ten Commandments—the commandments that God gave to His people, through Moses, that they are to follow if they want to be in right relationship with Him.[3] When the apostle Paul speaks about the Law in the New Testament, he routinely speaks of it as a command attached to a condition. In other words, Law is a demand within a conditional framework. This is why he selects Leviticus 18:5 (both in Gal. 3 and Rom. 10) as a summary of the salvation structure of the Law: if you keep the commandments, then you will live. The promise of life is linked to the condition of following the commandments and a corresponding threat for not following them: cursed is everyone who does not abide in all the things written in the Book of the Law, to do them (Gal. 3:10, citing Deut. 27:26). It is the condition that does the work of condemnation. Ifs kill!

Importantly, while every expression of Law contains an imperative, not all imperatives are necessarily Law. Let's say you're a pastor, and a college student comes to you for advice. He's worn-out because of the number of things he's involved in. He is in a fraternity, playing basketball, running track, waiting tables, and taking sixteen credit hours. The pressure he feels from his family to do it all and make something of himself is driving him crazy and wearing him down. After explaining his situation to you, you look at him and explain the Gospel—that because Jesus paid it all, we are free from the need to do it all. Our identity, worth, and value are not anchored in what we can accomplish but in what Jesus accomplished for us. Then you issue an imperative: "Now, quit track and drop one class." Does he hear this as bad news or good news? Good news, of course. The suggestion that he can let something go brings him much-needed relief—he can smell freedom. Like Galatians 5:1, the directive you issue the student is a directive not to submit to the slavery of a command with a condition (Law): "if you do more and try harder, you will make something of yourself and therefore find life." It is not a conditional imperative; it is an invitation. This is good news!

Or take an example from the Bible—that of the woman caught in adultery in John 8. Once the woman's accusers left, Jesus said to her, "Neither do I condemn you; go, and from now on sin no more" (v. 11) Does this final imperative disqualify the words of mercy? Is this a commandment with a condition? No! Otherwise Jesus would have instead said, "If you go and sin no more, then neither will I condemn you." But Jesus said, "Neither do I condemn you. Go and sin no more." The command is not a condition. "Neither do I condemn you" is categorical and unconditional; it comes with no strings attached. "Neither do I condemn you" creates an unconditional context within which "go and sin no more" is not an if. The only if the Gospel knows is this: "if anyone does sin, we have an advocate with the Father, Jesus Christ the righteous" (1 John 2:1).[4]

Next, like any standard of measurement, the Law measures. Meaning it provides a basis for sound judgment. If a scale tells us how heavy we are, the Law tells us how good we are. It quantifies. It ranks. It identifies. That is, because it makes a distinction between the righteous and the unrighteous, it has the power to tell us who we are. God's Law is like a mirror: it shows us who we really are and what we really need.

Third, the Law of God is inflexible. Jesus goes so far as to tell people to "be perfect, as your heavenly Father is perfect." Perfection is perfection. It does not compromise. Just like Urban Meyer's father, it accepts no excuses. It is written in stone—all or nothing, pure demand. We did not write it, so we can't revise it, much as we may like to. (It hasn't stopped us from trying!)

Fourth, the Law is universal. Lest we think it is something that applies only to Christians or people who take the Bible seriously, the Law is something that applies to all of creation, not just the ones who doff their hats to the Creator. And as we mentioned in the last chapter, Christ taught that the Law applies to motivation as well as action, our internal as well as our external lives.

Furthermore, and this is really important: the apostle Paul claimed the Law is written on the "fleshy tables" of the human heart (2 Cor. 3:3 KJV). What he meant is these shoulds and shouldn'ts are both instinctual and inescapable, part of our DNA. They are a psychological reality. We may justify our actions away, but deep down, we know when we've done something wrong.

BIG L'S AND LITTLE L'S

The great leader of the Protestant Reformation, Martin Luther, characterized the Law as "a voice that man can never stop in this life."

What he meant was that the voice of the Law expresses a demand that we, as sinful men and women, can never appease. It has a power of its own. Regardless of the form it takes this side of heaven, the function of the Law remains the same: it accuses.

Now, I know what you're thinking. *What does this have to do with one-way love and the exhaustion of life?* "I haven't committed adultery," you say. "I'm on good terms with my parents." Well, bear with me. Judgment and expectation lie at the bottom of much of the resentment, alienation, and rebellion we experience every day. What keeps you up at night may not be something you would classify as religious or spiritual; it may be the nagging fear of what another person thinks of you. Why haven't they called you back? Do they not like you? Are you not likeable? Do you not measure up? Perhaps you stay awake worrying about your job and all that you have to get done in the morning. If you don't get it done—and look good doing so—you won't get that promotion, and if you don't get that promotion, what will that mean about you? Are you a failure? A loser? So you run yourself ragged all day, making sure that your bases are covered.

Are you beginning to see? Our relationship with judgment and demand occupies an inordinate part of our headspace and lies at the root of so much stress and conflict. But this is also where we need to make a distinction, what I like to call the difference between big-L Law and little-l law. Big-L Law is the Law of God that we read about in the Bible. This big-L Law lies at the very heart of creation. It is so central to our existence, so ingrained in our hardwiring, that we see and hear echoes of it all over the place. We call these more everyday varieties little-l law. Paul Zahl puts it this way:

> Law with a small "l" refers to an interior principle
> of demand or ought that seems universal in human
> nature. In this sense, law is any voice that makes
> us feel we must do something or be something to
> merit the approval of another ... In daily living, law
> is an internalized principle of self-accusation. We
> might say that the innumerable laws we carry inside
> us are bastard children of the Law.[5]

Don't let the little *l* fool you—in impact, there is very little difference between the Law of God and the law we find in our culture. Just ask the teenage girl who feels that her body doesn't look like it should. Or the thirty-something woman torn between the simultaneous pressure to be a perfect mother and a successful career woman. These double standards are just as daunting and severe as the commands we find in the Bible. The only difference between big-L Law and little-l law is that one comes from the immutable mouth of God and the other arises out of the shifting sand of human enterprise. The masculine ideal that my sons are growing up with is different from the one I grew up with, but it is no less demanding. *If the big-L Law is good and holy, then little-l law is almost always arbitrary and cruel.*

I have tried my best to be consistent in usage throughout the book, with big-L Law referring to God's Law and little-l law the innumerable oughts of life. But the innumerable oughts of life often include big-L Law, so it is not always as cut-and-dried as it might seem. Not only do we, like the Pharisees in the Bible, tend to conflate the two in all sorts of subtle ways, we also tend to experience both forms in the same way—namely, as accusation and judgment. So while the content of one may be good and holy, and the content of the other may be fickle and demeaning—one may even be an inversion of the other—it seldom makes much of a difference to the one not measuring up. In other words, the point is not *how* we fall short of this standard or that standard, but *that* we invariably fall short.

One doesn't have to look far to find an ought; they are as ubiquitous as they are oppressive. For example, infomercials that promise a better life if you work at getting a better body, a neighbor's new car, the success of your coworker—all these things have the potential to communicate "you're not enough." Maybe you feel that you *have* to be on top of everything if you're going to make it; you *have* to infallibly protect your kids if they're going to turn out okay; you *have* to control what others think about you if you're going to feel important; you *have* to be the best if your life is going to count; you *have* to be successful if you're ever going to satisfy the deep desire for parental approval, and so on and so forth, world without end, amen.

People themselves can represent the law to us (and us to them!). For example, a particularly beautiful or successful person next to whom we can't help but feel inadequate. Or maybe a boss whose very presence makes us feel like we are not working hard enough, no matter how many hours we put in. They are *not* the law, but that is how we perceive them.

Not long ago, I was driving down the road near my house, and I passed a sign in front of a store that read, "Life is the art of drawing without an eraser." Meant to inspire drivers-by to work hard, live well, and avoid mistakes, it served as a booming voice of law to everyone that read it. "Don't mess up. There are no second chances. You had better get it right the first time."

The sad truth is, the world is full to the brim with laws. From the craziest communes of Portland, Oregon, to the sunniest streets of South Florida, from the straight-laced small towns of the Midwest to the untamed jungles of Paraguay, the law is a universal human reality. Conditionality is written into the fabric of every society and relationship because it is written into the fabric of every heart and mind (Rom. 2:15).

YOU KNOW YOU'RE A LAWYER WHEN ...

If you want to know where you're encountering the law, do a quick inventory of your fears. What are you afraid of? I mean, really afraid of? In their book *Stranger Than Fiction: When Our Minds Betray Us*, Drs. Marc and Jacqueline Feldman reference a survey of the general public that asked people the same thing. Death came in at number six. Number one, by a significant margin, was public speaking. I don't think it's much of a stretch to say that the fear of public speaking has more than a little to do with a deeper fear, the fear of judgment, of being the vulnerable focus of a roomful of people, all of whom are evaluating what you are saying and how you look. They may like you, or they may reject you.

The fear of judgment, arguably the deepest of all fears, creates much of the stress and depression of everyday life. And it derives a great deal of its power from the fact that, deep down, we all know we don't measure up and are, therefore, deserving of a guilty verdict. We are aware that we fail, that our best is never good enough, that we've been weighed in the balance and found wanting. One young mother recently put it as honestly as anyone can:

> Deep down, I know I should be perfect and I'm not. I feel it when someone comes into my house unannounced and there's a mess in every corner. I know it when my children misbehave in public and I just want to hide. I can tell it when that empty feeling rises after I've spoken in haste, said too much, or raised my voice. There's the feeling in my stomach that I just can't shake when I know I've missed the mark of perfection.

The judgment of others—social law, if you will—is a surface echo of a judgment that lies beneath. We are ultimately afraid of the judgment that the law wields. We instinctually know that if we don't measure up, the judge will punish us. When we feel this weight of judgment against us, we all tend to slip into the slavery of self-salvation: trying to appease the judge (friends, parents, spouse, ourselves) with hard work, good behavior, getting better, achievement, losing weight, and so on. We conclude, "If I can just stay out of trouble and get good grades, maybe my mom and dad will finally approve of me." "If I can overcome this addiction, then I'll be able to accept myself." "If I can get thin, maybe my husband will finally think I'm beautiful." "If I can make a name for myself and be successful, maybe I'll get the respect I long for." There are other responses to judgment that we will look at in the next chapter.

Suffice it to say, if there is an element of fear behind our everyday afflictions—workaholism, people pleasing, self-loathing, etc.—then the law is probably not far behind.

MIGHT AS WELL FACE IT, YOU'RE ADDICTED TO LAW

If it sounds like our relationship with the law is one-dimensional, let me assure you: it is not. The truth is, we are very conflicted. We may dislike being told what to do, we may hate being judged, but as we learned in the last chapter, we *love* being in control. And the law, at least on the surface, assures us that we determine our own destiny. As the great Scottish churchman Ralph Erskine so beautifully wrote, "The law could promise life to me, if my obedience perfect be."[6]

This we understand. This we like. The outcome of our lives remains firmly in our hands. "Give me five principles for raising exemplary children, and I can guarantee myself a happy family if I just obey those five principles." If we can do certain things, meet certain standards (whether God's, our own, our parents', our spouse's, society's, whomever's), and become a certain way, then we'll make it. It feels like it works—at least that's what we've been told. Conditionality lets us feel safe, because it breeds a sense of manageability. The equation "*If* I do this, *then* you are obligated to do that" keeps life formulaic and predictable, and more important, it keeps the earning power in our camp.

People who are addicted to control are addicted to the law as a means of control. And this sadly applies to Christians as well as non-Christians. In fact, far too many churches are completely in thrall to the law, so much so that most of the non-Christians you meet will describe Christianity as a religion of law. They may not use those terms, but listen closely, and what you'll hear, almost without fail, has to do with rules and judgment. As Walter Marshall says in his book *The Gospel Mystery of Sanctification*, "By nature, you are completely addicted to a legal method of salvation. Even after you become a Christian by believing the Gospel, your heart is still addicted to salvation by works … You find it hard to believe that you should get any blessing before you work for it."[7]

Against this tumult of conditionality—punishment and reward, scorekeeping, you-get-what-you-deserve, big-L Law, little-l law, whatever name you choose—comes the second of God's two words: His grace, His one-way love. Grace is the gift that has no strings attached. It is what makes the Good News so good, the once-and-for-all so that we may be free. Ironically, though, this amazing word of relief can be offensive to us.

I'll never forget hearing Dr. Doug Kelly (one of my theology professors in seminary) say in class, "If you want to make people mad, preach law. If you want to make them really, really mad, preach grace." I didn't know what he meant then. But I do now.

The law offends us because it tells us what to do—and most of the time, we hate anyone telling us what to do. But ironically, grace offends us even more, because it tells us that there is nothing we *can* do, that everything has already been done. And if there is something we hate more than being told what to do, it's being told that we can't do anything, that we can't earn anything—that we are helpless, weak, and needy.

However much we hate the law, we are more afraid of grace. Because we are natural-born do-it-yourselfers, the vitriolic reaction to unconditional grace is understandable. Grace generates panic, because it wrestles both control and glory out of our hands. This means that the part of you that gets angry and upset and mean and defensive and slanderous and critical and skeptical and feisty when you hear about God's one-way love is the very part of you that is still enslaved.

The Gospel of grace announces that Jesus came to acquit the guilty. He came to judge and be judged in our place. Christ came to satisfy the deep accusation against us once and for all so that we can be free from the judgment of God, others, and ourselves. He came to relieve us of our endlessly exhausting efforts at trying to deal with judgment on our own. The Gospel declares that our guilt has been atoned for, the Law has been fulfilled. So we don't need to live under the burden of trying to appease the judgment we feel; in Christ, the ultimate demand has been met, the deepest judgment has been satisfied. The internal voice that says, "Do this and live" gets drowned out by the external voice that says, "It is finished!"

But I am getting ahead of myself.

URBAN MEYER IS DEAD; LONG LIVE URBAN MEYER

After Urban Meyer's very public collapse, he took some time off. He went on a road trip with his son. He attended his daughter's volleyball games. He made peace with his father. He even rediscovered the reason he got into football in the first place: love of the game. Eventually he took a new position as coach for Ohio State, and above his new desk he hung his contract—not the contract he signed with the university, but the one he signed with his wife and children—the one that prioritized his family and his health. An expression of love rather than judgment. It's a beautiful story, and it's not over.

An article about Urban during his transition mentions a book he used to live by, written for business executives, called *Change or Die*. He has talked about the book in speeches, given away countless copies, invited the author to meet with his teams, but never did he realize the book described him down to a tee. The article recounts an episode that occurred in the car on the way to Cleveland, in which someone read Urban a passage from the book:

> "Why do people persist in their self-destructive behavior, ignoring the blatant fact that what they've been doing for many years hasn't solved their problems? They think that they need to do it even more fervently or frequently, as if they were doing the right thing but simply had to try even harder."
>
> Meyer's voice changes, grows firmer, louder. "Blatant fact," he says.
>
> He pauses. A fragmented idea orders itself in his mind. "Wow," he says.
>
> He asks to hear it again. "Blatant fact," he says. "It should have my picture. I need to read that to my wife. I'm gonna reread that now. Self-destructive behavior?"[8]

This is a man who was addicted to the law, so much so that it destroyed him. Yet his defeat turned out not to be the end he feared it would be but the beginning of something new, the advent of a man finally free enough from the stranglehold of narcissistic performancism that he could not only laugh at himself but begin to love those around him. Self-destruction was not the end of his story; neither is the Law the end of ours. It is the first word, but thank God it's not the last. The last word is the one that comes straight from the mouth of Jesus himself when he says, "For God did not send his Son into the world to condemn the world, but to save the world through him" (John 3:17 NIV).

CHAPTER 4

I FOUGHT THE LAW (AND THE LAW WON)

Kim and I were twenty-one when we got married. We met when we were nineteen, right in the middle of my "wilderness period," and because we were so rebellious—me more than her—we brought quite a bit of baggage into our relationship. Those first five years were rough. Not abusive or anything, but I can distinctly remember wanting to hit the eject button on a number of occasions. The source of the friction was always one of two things: 1. I expected her to be a certain way, and she wasn't meeting my expectations. 2. She expected me to be a certain way, and I wasn't meeting her expectations. We were so hard on each other in those early years! Especially me. It makes me cringe to even think about all I put this incredible woman through.

Both of us were brand-new Christians at the time, which you might think would have provided a solid foundation for our relationship. But because I had grown up in a Christian home and she hadn't, and because I had gone through such a wild period of living, I was a very legalistic young believer. It's not uncommon for people who have recently undergone a conversion to experience an overzealous phase. In my case, I was trying to protect myself from going back to what I used to be. I wrongly concluded that, although I had been saved and pursued by God's grace, it was now up to me to erect stringent boundaries and lay down the law on myself and everyone around me—only then would I be able to avoid the pain and self-destructiveness I had experienced before. I had wrongly concluded that my problems were circumstantial or due to outside factors. As long as I could avoid substances, women, and Johnny Law, my relationship with God was safe. Of course, while boundaries and law can curtail some of that stuff, my real problem was inside, and the law unfortunately can't do anything about that. In fact, as we'll explore in this chapter, it may even make things worse.

I put some heavy demands on both Kim and myself in those early years. We laugh about it now, but back then it wasn't so funny. Most of it had to do with our spiritual life. I can remember being particularly strict about reading the Bible. So much so that if I woke up and read one chapter instead of three, I would feel miserable all day long. Even worse, I would project that same standard onto Kim, making her feel small and inadequate if she didn't wake up and have a lengthy quiet time first thing in the morning. *Barefoot in the Park* it was not!

I was also absurdly uptight about not doing anything recreational on Sunday. If she wanted to go out and do something as innocuous as plant flowers, from my seat on the couch where I was watching sports, I would give her a withering look (pun intended) that said, "Shame, shame, I know your name.... First, it's flowers on the Sabbath; next, you'll be wanting to *exercise*!"

And then there was the whole realm of parenting, always an extremely ripe area for judgment and scorekeeping. Kim did not grow up in a religious home, so her mother and father never put her to bed and prayed with her, never read a picture Bible with her. I remember when our son Gabe was little and it would come time to put him to bed, Kim would walk into his room, put him down in his crib, and walk out. I'd be sitting there—not helping but ready with a million questions (that weren't really questions). "Did you not pray with him, pray over him, sing a song to him? No 'Jesus Loves Me'?" I'm sure Kim was extremely grateful that the bedtime police were on the case.

Possibly the most embarrassing moments, looking back, came during the hour-long prayer sessions I would insist on each night. We would keep extensive journals with long lists of thanksgiving and people to pray for—which, on the surface, is a wonderful thing. But that was just the beginning. I would strongly recommend that we get on our knees to pray (because everyone knows that God is more pleased when we pray on our knees). And I would typically go first, praying these long, lofty prayers. Kim would be scared to go next. She was afraid that she would say the wrong thing, or even if she said the right thing, that she wouldn't say it eloquently enough. Because it was typically late at night when we would pray together, she would sometimes fall asleep during my prayer. I would gently wake her and condescendingly remind her about the time Jesus asked his disciples to stay up and pray on the night he was arrested only to discover them sleeping when he returned from his private prayer to the Father. We laugh so hard about that now. But it wasn't funny then.

I put so much pressure on her. I made her feel like a second-class citizen. She was spiritually blue-collar, I was spiritually white-collar, and she had a lot of growing up to do if she was going to get to *my* level.

In my infinite wisdom, I would even compare her to my mother—lesson number one of what *not* to do when you are a young married couple! My mother, of course, wasn't just any woman. As far as I was concerned, she and my grandmother were the embodiment of godliness, the gold standard of what a Christian wife and mother should be. How could Kim possibly measure up to that? She soon began to feel insecure, both as a person and in our relationship. When she picked up the Bible, even though she often didn't understand what she was reading, she would do it because she was afraid I would look down on her if she didn't. Our actions may have looked holy to an outside observer, but underneath, we were operating out of fear and guilt rather than faith and grace. No wonder we were so unhappy. It is a testament to both the grace of God and Kim's own incredible character and beauty that she stuck with me.

Those early years turned out to be an extended lesson in what the law can do to a relationship. We learned firsthand that relational demand creates relational detachment, that judgment has the power to kill love. And you don't have to be religious to find that out! The impossible demands in our relationship were soaked in Christian language and practice, but that was simply our context. I've seen husbands and wives who are hard on each other about the most ridiculous things, from the way they chew their food to the way their voice sounds when they're speaking on the phone to the type of presents they give each other. Kim and I may not have been yelling and screaming at each other, but our marriage was relationally rocky during that time. The fruit of judgment proved to be unbearable amounts of self-righteousness on my part and crippling amounts of insecurity and fear in her. It's a good thing God intervened!

FIGHT, FLIGHT, AND APPEASEMENT

Most parents and spouses, siblings and friends—even preachers—fall prey to the illusion that real change happens when we lay down the law, exercise control, demand good performance, or offer "constructive" criticism. We wonder why our husbands grow increasingly withdrawn over the years, why our children don't call as much as we would like them to, why our colleagues don't confide in us, why our congregants become relationally and emotionally detached from us. In more cases than not, it happens because we are feeding their deep fear of judgment—by playing the judge. Our lips may be moving, but the voice they hear is that of the law. The law may have the power to instruct and expose, but it does not have the power to inspire or create.

Think about it in terms of when you've encountered some form of accusing demand from another person. The gap between who we are and who we should be always produces a reaction. If we're criticized, we defend. If we're rejected, we sulk. It's never neutral. When we feel this weight of judgment against us, those who are addicted to their own sense of control—all of us—tend to slip into the slavery of self-salvation. Our three most common and instinctual self-salvation strategies are fight, flight, or appeasement. All of them are consuming, but none is particularly productive. The opposite, in fact.

Perhaps your instinct is to fight. You know the judge isn't leaving anytime soon, but you're not either, so you put up your dukes. As my friend Ethan Richardson writes, "You bicker with your boss about his unrealistic expectations, condescend about the *vanity* of going to the gym, blame your parents for what they've done to you, or wear leather and turn the speakers up."[1]

Maybe you spend your time and energy trying to demolish whatever system you feel judged by, telling yourself that right and wrong are just social constructs and you see through them. Or maybe you are so sensitive to criticism that every interaction becomes a power struggle, and you can never let your guard down. But the law is bigger than we are—it will win every time. That is simply its nature.

Maybe your response is flight. You run from whatever standard you perceive to be accusing you. You leave home and travel the world. You stop answering *their* phone calls. You close your eyes and cover your ears and maybe even change your name. You'd be surprised how often this happens. I'll never forget an experience at summer camp. A good friend got in trouble for some inappropriate behavior and was sent home. When we got back, a number of us reached out to see how he was doing. None of us ever heard from him again. We'd all come to represent the condemnation he experienced. Whatever form it takes, the idea is: the judge isn't going anywhere, so I will. Sayonara!

Then there's appeasement, probably the most popular path. The judge (friends, parents, spouse, ourselves) has found us wanting in some way, so we beg and plead and show him how hard we are trying. We tell him we're sorry, promising that we'll do better next time. Appeasement involves cowering before the judge, hoping at some point he/she/it might understand and sympathize with our situation. We try to appease the judge's demands with hard work, good behavior, impressive achievements, and so on. We conclude, "If I can make a name for myself and be successful, maybe I'll get the respect I long for." "If I lose ten pounds and buy some new clothes, maybe my husband will finally think I'm beautiful and pay attention to me." "If I help out more with the kids, maybe my wife won't criticize me as much." We buy into the delusion that we are capable of silencing (or reasoning with) that voice of demand.

The problem with fight, flight, and appeasement is not so much that they're unwise, but that they don't work. No matter how angry or strong or committed, no fighter can beat those granite tablets into a more manageable shape and size. Like anyone who spends their time punching a brick wall, fighters end up bitter, bruised, and alone.

Flight may work for a while. We may experience some relief from the external accusation we feel from a family member or church official. But we are almost always dismayed to discover that our problems have followed us. Our guilt before the law is not circum-stantial, after all. It goes much deeper. We carry it with us wherever we go. I thought all my problems would be solved by getting out from under my parents and teachers, but I was dead wrong!

Finally, those who go the appeasement route, which is most of us, find that no amount of hard work, nice gestures, phone calls, or good works is ever enough. Appeasement, like people-pleasing, is a despair-producing process. If we're living in an environment or we are in a relationship that feeds the fear of judgment with constant criticism, we deflate and detach because it becomes discouragingly exhausting trying to satisfy the demands and appease the judgment of the other. We become depleted of the hope that we can ever attain the affirmation that seems so necessary for us to live and breathe, and so the relationship flounders. How much money is enough, Mr. Rockefeller? Just a little bit more …

In his book *Who Will Deliver Us?* Paul Zahl writes:

> I wonder if any of us are strong enough to with-stand the perceived judgments upon our lives, which touch the fears within. Have you ever tried to win the favor of a person who actively dislikes you? To get him to like you, you may have changed your style of dress. You may have altered your schedule. You may have stopped something you've been doing or started something new. You may have carried out their wishes to the last detail. You may have tried once, then again, then a thousand times. But you have not won from this person the

affirmation you so deeply desire. Judgment steam-rolls over most of us.[2]

WALKING AWAY SORROWFUL

Let's shift gears for a moment. Perhaps you are familiar with Jesus's interaction with the rich young ruler. It is a remarkable case study in the nature of the Law and our response to it:

> And as [Jesus] was setting out on his journey, a man ran up and knelt before him and asked him, "Good Teacher, what must I do to inherit eternal life?" And Jesus said to him, "Why do you call me good? No one is good except God alone. You know the commandments: 'Do not murder, Do not commit adultery, Do not steal, Do not bear false witness, Do not defraud, Honor your father and mother.'" And he said to him, "Teacher, all these I have kept from my youth." And Jesus, looking at him, loved him, and said to him, "You lack one thing: go, sell all that you have and give to the poor, and you will have treasure in heaven; and come, follow me." Disheartened by the saying, he went away sorrowful, for he had great possessions. (Mark 10:17–22)

The rich young ruler approached Jesus with quite a question: "What must I do to inherit eternal life?" It may sound lofty and arcane, but it's a question we are all very familiar with, one that we ask all the time. What is the right way to live? What *should* I do if I want to be a good person/father/Christian? Jesus naturally reiterates the Law of God, the divine standard of goodness and righteousness. The young man must be an appeaser, because he shoots back an answer that would leave most modern people speechless. He claims that he has kept all the commandments since his youth! The self-righteousness jumps off the page and is painful to read, especially since it's so reminiscent of how I used to treat my poor Kim. A life lived according to the law breeds self-righteousness.

Christ knows that "no one is good"— appeasement is not possible, as no man is free of sin—so he says the one thing that will make the young man realize the gap between who he should be and who he actually is. He goes for the jugular: the young man's pocketbook. His pocketbook is the sum of his worldly achievements, very likely something the young man is proud of. Christ knows that his money is emblematic of his self-salvation strategy, so he aims the hammer of the Law and brings it down, telling this poor guy to sell it all and give the money to the poor. Notice how the young man responds. Is he inspired to take the plunge and give it all away? No! He becomes sorrowful and leaves. The Law has exposed him as the sinner he is, a man unwilling to give up control over his life and soul, and this is not happy news. The information Christ provides him with does not translate into action. Correction: it prompts him to walk away with his head hanging Charlie Brown–style, to distance himself from the Lawgiver. He moves in the opposite direction. This is the key insight we find in the Bible about the nature of the Law (and demand and exhortation, etc.): *it does not and cannot produce its intended effect.* So what does it produce if not what it intends?

The apostle Paul notes that the giving of the Law to Israel did not lead to a newfound obedience but began a history of rebellion that he can even see in himself (Rom. 7:7–9; 9:30–32). Jesus's severe indictment of the Jewish leaders in the New Testament does not lead to a heartfelt repentance, but to his own crucifixion. Jesus's command to his disciples that they must take up their crosses and follow him fails to get their martyr juices flowing. Instead, they all abandon him. Paul's stinging criticism of the Corinthians leads directly to his own tearful letter in 2 Corinthians 10–13. In each instance, the arrival of the Law does not lead to life but to disobedience and death. And I haven't even mentioned the most obvious example of all, the very first one, in the Garden of Eden. The command not to eat from the Tree of Good and Evil prompts Adam and Eve to disobey rather than follow it. If the Law has a purpose, it may just be this paradoxical outcome.

THE FRUIT OF THE LAW: RESENTMENT, REBELLION, AND EXHAUSTION

In 2012, *The Guardian* published an excoriating email sent by retired Royal Navy officer Nick Crews to his son and two daughters.[3] It quickly became a viral sensation. The letter lists, in remarkably colorful language, all the misery that the three grown children had put their father and mother through, from failed marriages and careers to poor finances to fears about their grandchildren's well-being. The final paragraph is particularly vicious:

I can now tell you that I for one, and I sense Mum feels the same, have had enough of being forced to live through the never-ending bad dream of our children's underachievement and domestic ineptitudes. I want to hear no more from any of you until, if you feel inclined, you have a success or an achievement or a REALISTIC plan for the support and happiness of your children to tell me about. I don't want to see your mother burdened any more with your miserable woes— it's not as if any of the advice she strives to give you has ever been listened to with good grace—far less acted upon. So I ask you to spare her further unhappiness. If you think I have been unfair in what I have said, by all means try to persuade me to change my mind. But you won't do it by simply whingeing and saying you don't like it. You'll have to come up with meaty reasons to demolish my points and build a case for yourself. If that isn't possible, or you simply can't be bothered, then I rest my case.

I am bitterly, bitterly disappointed.

Dad

Wow! Any parent can relate to Mr. Crews's frustration. And many of us can probably relate to his children and the disapproval they must have felt. It does not sound like Mr. Crews is making things up. He and his wife apparently have every reason to be so bitterly disappointed and angry. Like the Law itself, the content of his missive may be well-founded, and their standards for their children may be perfectly reasonable (and righteous). But expectations, as they say, are planned resentments; law and bitterness are frequent bedfellows. We expect people not to be self-centered sinners, and when they turn out to be just that, we get angry and blame them!

Do you think that the letter had the effect Mr. Crews intended? Absolutely not! I don't care who you are, no one responds to a letter like that by saying, "By golly, Dad, thanks for pointing these things out. Now that I know how much pain we've caused and how irresponsible we've been, starting tomorrow, that's all over." Of course, the law may work … for a little while. Guilt and fear can be powerful motivators in the short run. What they cannot do is change a heart from self-seeking to self-sacrificing. The letter may have succeeded in scaring the kids straight for a spell, but fear of further berating would be the driving factor, not the genuine desire to fly right. What's much more likely is that the children would be so hurt and offended that they struck back at their father by releasing his letter to an international media outlet, so that he might be castigated and humiliated by the public. Which is precisely what happened. His email backfired. Instead of bringing his children closer, it pushed them further away. This is an echo of what the apostle Paul meant when he wrote that "the law was brought in so that the trespass might increase" (Rom. 5:20 NIV).

It makes me sad that some pastors invoke Mr. Crews's tactics from the pulpit. Frustrated with their congregation's failure to come to church enough, get involved enough, give enough money, pray enough, read their Bibles enough, invite their friends enough, so many pastors use their position to send verbal letters. "How can you afford your fancy SUV but not give more to the church? How can you take your kid to their soccer game every Sunday but never bring them to youth group?" Pastors who resent their congregations are just like husbands who resent their wives—the resulting guilt may produce some modified behavior for a while, but estrangement and rebellion are inevitable. The only difference is that a congregation has every right to expect that their pastor will preach a little Good News every Sunday. Make no mistake: over time, preachers who major on law and behavior rather than grace and faith will empty their pews and create refugees. Human DNA simply cannot bear the weight of the law indefinitely.

Pulpits today are full of preachers telling one-legged people to jump higher and run faster. Musician Rich Mullins once wrote, "I have attended church regularly since I was less than a week old. I've listened to sermons about virtue, sermons against vice. I have heard about money, time management, tithing, abstinence, and generosity. I've listened to thousands of sermons. But I could count on one hand the number [of sermons] that were a simple proclamation of the Gospel of Christ."[4]

It's not just Rich. I received the following letter recently from someone I've never met. He wrote:

Over the last couple of years, we have really been struggling with the preaching in our church as it has been very law laden and moralistic. After listening, I feel condemned with no power to overcome my lack of ability to obey. Over the last several months, I have found myself very spiritually depressed, to the point where I had no desire to even attend church. Pastors are so concerned about somehow preaching "too much grace" (as if that is possible), because they wrongly believe that type of preaching leads to antinomianism or licentiousness. But, I can testify that the opposite is actually true. I believe preaching only the law and giving little to no gospel actually leads to lawless living. When mainly law is preached, it leads to the realization that I can't follow it, so I might as well quit trying. At least, that's what has happened to me.

So sad. And frustrating. The ironic thing about legalism is that it not only doesn't make people work harder, it makes them give up. Moralism doesn't produce morality; rather, it produces immorality. *The Onion* brilliantly parodied this dynamic with its article, "Where Are All These 'Loose Women' My Pastor Keeps Warning Me About?," in which a fictional seventeen-year-old kid laments that he never seems to run into any of the promiscuous ladies that he hears about at church so often.[5] The humor is based in reality. It is no coincidence, for example, that the straight-laced *Leave It to Beaver* generation preceded the free-love movement of the 1960s. We live in a country where the state most known for its wholesomeness and frugality, Utah, also leads the country in rates of pornography consumption and antidepressant prescriptions.[6]

We make a big mistake when we conclude that the law is the answer to bad behavior. In fact, the law alone *stirs up* more of such behavior. People get worse, not better, when you lay down the law. This isn't to say the Spirit doesn't use both God's Law and God's Gospel in our lives and for our good. But the Law and the Gospel do very different things. The Law reveals sin but is powerless to remove it. It points to righteousness but can't produce it. It shows us what godliness is, but it cannot make us godly. As Martin Luther wrote, "Sin is not canceled by lawful living, for no person is able to live up to the Law. Nothing can take away sin except the grace of God."⁷ The Law apart from the Gospel can only crush; it cannot cure.

WHY THEN THE LAW?

If you are at all like me, at this point you must be asking, "What is the purpose of the Law if it doesn't seem to be able to produce what it calls for? If the fruit of the Law is self-righteousness, rebellion, resentment, and ultimately death, why bother with it at all? Are you saying that the Law is indeed bad?" No! The answer comes in Jesus's words to his disciples after the rich young ruler walked away sorrowful:

> And Jesus looked around and said to his disciples, "How difficult it will be for those who have wealth to enter the kingdom of God!" And the disciples were amazed at his words. But Jesus said to them again, "Children, how difficult it is to enter the kingdom of God! It is easier for a camel to go through the eye of a needle than for a rich person to enter the kingdom of God." And they were exceedingly astonished, and said to him, "Then who can be saved?" Jesus looked at them and said, "With man it is impossible, but not with God. For all things are possible with God." (Mark 10:23–27)

Can you see what Jesus was up to? Before that young man could look outside himself for help, he needed to be disillusioned about who he was. The Law, to paraphrase Martin Luther, is a divine Hercules sent to attack and kill the monster of self-righteousness—a monster that continues to harass the redeemed. We need the Law to freshly reveal to us that we are worse off than we think we are. We need to be reminded that there is something to be pardoned even in our best works and proudest achievements.[8]

But then, once we are recrushed by Law, we need to be reminded that "there is a fountain fill'd with blood drawn from Immanuel's veins, and sinners plunged beneath that flood lose all their guilty stains" (W. Cowper). We need to be told that the sins we cannot forget, God cannot remember, or as the old hymn puts it, that "though th' accuser roar, of ills that I have done, I know them all and thousands more; Jehovah findeth none." We need to be told over and over that there is no condemnation for those who are in Christ Jesus, that nothing can separate us from God's love, and that Christians live their lives under a banner that reads, "It is finished."

The Gospel declares that Jesus came not to abolish the Law, but to fulfill it. Jesus met all of God's holy conditions so that our relationship with God could be wholly unconditional. The demand maker became a demand keeper and died for me—a demand breaker.

Until we realize that self-salvation is *impossible*, we will not be interested in the One with whom all things are *possible*. In its mirrorlike fashion, the Law reveals our helplessness before the devastation and comprehensiveness of divine expectation, and that helplessness creates the space for God's amazing grace and the freedom it produces. It shows us who we really are, stripping away every shred of our self-justifying and delusional facades. In doing so, it leaves us no other option than to cling to the One who has fulfilled the Law in our place. I wish I could say I do everything for God's glory. I can't. Neither can you. What I can say is Jesus' blood covers all my efforts to glorify myself. I wish I could say Jesus fully satisfies me. I can't. Neither can you. What I can say is Jesus fully satisfied God for me.

This happy exchange lies at the very heart of what the Bible teaches about Christ. He did for us what we could not do for ourselves, not just acting in a righteous way, but *being* righteousness himself—so that we might become the righteousness of God. This is why the Gospel is such good news to those who have failed in significant ways. It offers more than a second chance to get things right, it offers a substitute. God, in fact, is not the God of second chances. He is the God of one chance and a second Adam. Perhaps my favorite illustration of our relationship to the Law in Christ is the following:

> [We are] a little like the duck hunter who was hunting with his friend in a wide-open barren of land in southeastern Georgia. Far away on the horizon he noticed a cloud of smoke. Soon, he could hear the sound of crackling. A wind came up and he realized the terrible truth: a brush fire was advancing his way. It was moving so fast that he and his friend could not outrun it. The hunter began to rifle through his pockets. Then he emptied all the contents of his knapsack. He soon found what he

was looking for—a book of matches. To his friend's amazement, he pulled out a match and struck it. He lit a small fire around the two of them. Soon they were standing in a circle of blackened earth, waiting for the brush fire to come. They did not have to wait long. They covered their mouths with their handkerchiefs and braced themselves. The fire came near—and swept over them. But they were completely unhurt. They weren't even touched. Fire would not burn the place where fire had already burned.[9]

The point here is that the Law is like a brush fire that takes no prisoners. It cannot be escaped or extinguished or circumvented. But if we stand in the burned-over place, where Law has already done its worst, we will not get hurt. Its power has not been nullified, nor has its necessity and authority been denied. Yet because of where we are standing, not a hair on our heads will be singed. The death of Christ is the burned-over place. There we huddle, hardly believing yet relieved. Christ's death has disarmed the Law, and where there was once guilt, now all that remains is gratitude.

Again, just think about your own life for a moment. As much as we might wish the world—and we ourselves—didn't operate according to debits and credits, there is always a cost to what we do. We are conditional beings living in a conditional universe. "I called you last time, now it's your turn to call me." "If you lie to me, there must be an apology before we're good again." The condition must be met, the cost must be paid—"either I swallow my pride, you say you're sorry, or we never talk to each other again." But the debt has to go somewhere. Christianity alone affirms that the God who makes the demands also met those demands for us in the person of Jesus. That God would deign to reach us in a way that both acknowledges and resolves these fundamental realities is not juvenile or overly abstract/economic—it is both gracious and miraculous. We are both fully known and fully loved.

I NEED A MIRACLE EVERY DAY

Looking back, the root of Kim and my marriage problems those first few years wasn't that I was too focused on the Law—the problem was that I wasn't focused on it enough! J. Gresham Machen counterintuitively notes that "a low view of law always produces legalism; a high view of law makes a person a seeker after grace."[10] The reason this seems so counterintuitive is because most people think that those who talk a lot about grace have a low view of God's Law (hence, the regular charge of antinomianism, that is, of preaching in such a way as to imply that the Law is bad and/or useless). Others think that those with a high view of the Law are the legalists. But Machen makes the very compelling point that it's a low view of the Law that produces legalism, because a low view of the Law causes us to conclude that we can do it—the bar is low enough for us to jump over. A low view of the Law makes us think that the standards are attainable, the goals are reachable, the demands are doable. The Law gets softened into "helpful tips for practical living" instead of God's unwavering demand for absolute perfection. It's this low view of the Law that caused Immanuel Kant—and Pelagius before him—to conclude that "ought implies can." That is, to say, "that I ought to do something is to imply logically that I am able to do it."

A high view of the Law, however, demolishes all notions that we can do it—it exterminates all attempts at self-sufficient moral endeavor. We'll always maintain a posture of suspicion regarding the radicality of unconditional grace as long as we think we have the capacity to pull it off. Only an inflexible picture of what God demands is able to penetrate the depth of our need and convince us that we never outgrow our need for grace—that grace never gets overplayed.

Contrary to what some Christians today would have you believe, the biggest problem facing the church today is not "cheap grace" but "cheap Law"—the idea that God accepts anything less than the perfect righteousness of Jesus. My friend John Dink explains cheap Law this way:

> Cheap law weakens God's demand for perfection, and in doing so, breathes life into ... [our] quest for a righteousness of [our] own making.... It creates people of great zeal, but they lack knowledge concerning the question "What Would Jesus Do?" Here is the costly answer: Jesus would do it all perfectly. And that's game over for you. The Father is not grooming you to be a replacement for his Beloved Son. He is announcing that there is blessing for those who take shelter *in his Beloved Son*. Cheap law tells us that we've fallen, but there's good news, you can get back up again.... Therein lies

the great heresy of cheap law: it is a false gospel. It
cheapens—no—it nullifies grace.[11]

Only when we understand that God's Law is absolutely inflexible
will we see that God's grace is absolutely indispensible. A high view
of the Law involves the devastating reminder that God's acceptance
of us is ultimately contingent on Christ's perfection, not our progress; Christ's imputation, not our improvement. Such inscrutable
demands push us toward the infallible deliverance we find in the
Gospel. In other words, a high view of the Law produces a high view
of grace. A low view of the Law produces a low view of grace.

In my early years of being married, I had mistakenly concluded
that by checking the various behavior boxes, I could keep my past
(and the pain of the past) at bay. That by spiritually disciplining
myself (and forcing Kim to do the same), I could straighten myself
out and manipulate God into keeping me safe and inside His good
graces. I didn't realize that the spirit with which I was going through
the motions—the spirit of earning and control—was just as grave a
transgression as anything I had been doing before, if not worse. All
the quiet times in the world don't amount to a hill of beans when it
comes to justifying ourselves before a Holy God. I was yet another
tired actor trying to be the director and watching as those I cared
about most suffered the brunt of that illusion. It is truly a testament
to God's mercy that they persevered with me. They even spared me
any harshly worded letters.

CHAPTER 5

EX-CONVICTS, FAILED DISCIPLES, AND ONE-WAY LOVE

There wasn't one thing in particular that snapped me out of my "wild man" phase, no big crisis or single clarifying moment that inspired me to repair the damage I had done to myself, others, and my family. As humdrum as it may sound, what led me out of that rebellious period was simply the nagging sense that there had to be more to life than what I was experiencing—there had to be more to who I was than what this world was telling me. In fact, I can't even pinpoint the exact moment when God raised this dead rebel to life. All I know is that sometime in the fall of 1993, my culminating discontent with life made me decide to start going back to church.

I was twenty-one at the time. Kim, who had been my girl-friend for two years at that point, had actually started going to church with my parents a few months earlier, and before I knew it, we were both going every week. My parents were understand-ably overjoyed. Their prodigal had finally come home. "For this son of mine was dead and is alive again; he was lost and is found" (Luke 15:24 NIV).

Since Kim did not grow up in a Christian home like me, this was all brand-new to her. But to me, it felt like a homecoming. Even in my unruly years, I had never really ceased to believe in God. In fact, if you had given me a theological exam at the height of my rebellion, I would've passed with flying colors. I was just choosing to ignore it all. Maybe it was the timing, maybe it was the circumstances, but something finally clicked, and God became real to both of us in a new and exciting way.

About three months later, in January of 1994, Kim and I got engaged. Our new faith naturally led us to take a hard look at our relationship. God was changing us, and we knew our relationship needed to change as well. After being so out of control for so long, we knew we had to adjust the way we related to each other, and the physical realm was no exception. We were both coming out of a world where sex outside of marriage was completely the norm—a norm that we had embraced—and we knew the right thing to do would be to pull back until we were married. Easier said than done! Despite our best intentions and most earnest efforts, we slipped up three or four times during our engagement.

I'll never forget when Kim came over to my apartment one night after work and told me she was pregnant. I was devastated. Not just because the news was a shock or because I hadn't expected to be a parent at such a young age. I was devastated because everyone who had celebrated my return "to the fold" would think the turnaround was a false alarm. I had caused my family so much pain and heartbreak with my self-absorbed shenanigans, and they had been so relieved and excited that their reckless son had finally come back; it had been the answer to years and years of prayer. I had put my parents through more than any son ever should and had asked for their forgiveness on numerous occasions. To drop this bomb might crush them all over again, and I just couldn't bear it. I was scared, ashamed, and angry at myself for failing yet again.

Somehow we summoned the courage to go over to my mom and dad's house the next day—Mother's Day, believe it or not. After some awkward small talk, I asked my father if we could speak to him alone. We walked out to the driveway. Dad was standing in front of me, and Kim was by my side, shoulder to shoulder.

"Dad we have something to tell you." I burst into tears. "Kim's pregnant."

Kim started bawling too. Next thing I knew, he was embracing both of us, me with one arm, her with the other, while we wept. He held us for ten minutes. He could see how overwhelmed we were. I can still hear his voice telling us, "It's okay. We love you. It's going to be okay. This child is going to be a blessing."

Kim and I had been so excited about getting married, and now we were going to be parents as well. In addition to the embarrassment and shame involved, we were grieving the happy expectation that we'd have a few years, just the two of us, before starting a family. We were in a state of shock. Yet my father did not condemn or lecture us, even though he had every right to do so. Instead, he comforted us. More than that, he gave us good news. He told us that while the circumstances clearly weren't ideal, this was going to turn out just fine. This baby was going to be a blessing to both of us and a gift to the whole family. Every time Kim and I look at our oldest son (now eighteen), we realize afresh that my dad was absolutely right that day.

The whole situation was wrapped in grace: I deserved his reproach and disapproval—premarital sex resulting in unexpected pregnancy is no father's dream for his child—yet his gracious response assured me that he not only wasn't crushed, his love for me was stronger than ever. When I told him (through many tears) how sorry I was for once again letting him down, he simply hushed me by hugging me tighter and saying over and over again, "It's okay. I love you. It's okay. I love you." At that moment in the driveway, when I rightly deserved my dad's disappointment, he assured me of his delight.

Even now it is hard to put into words the emotional relief I felt. *Lifesaving* is not too strong a word. I thank God with every fiber of my being that He put me in a family where I was surrounded by such one-way love.

The love my father showed me that day is not a one-to-one approximation of God's one-way love for you and me—nothing is! In fact, before we go any further, I should clarify: the Gospel is the announcement of Jesus Christ given for and to sinners. It refers to the one true act of Grace, or one-way love, to which all others point. Like small-l law, small-g grace refers to the infinite reflections or echoes or outworkings of big-G Grace we see and experience in relationships, art, etc.

My father was not preaching the Gospel to me that day—he didn't sit me down to tell me that, on account of Christ, my sins were forgiven. Instead, he showed me grace. That is, he treated me in a way that was analogous to how God treats you and me. He was not God, of course, but like many fathers, he did play a similar role in my life: someone in authority who showed me love in the midst of deserved judgment. As it is with big-L and little-l law, if occasionally we use big-G and little-g grace interchangeably, it is not because they are the same thing, but because we often experience them that way.

So what is grace exactly? There are three things about my interaction in the driveway that day that point to the essence of grace, or one-way love. First, one-way love has nothing to do with the beloved—in that case, me. It has to do with the one doing the loving—in that case, my father. I was at my least lovable in that instance—a repeat offender whose offense was going to have very real consequences—yet somehow my father treated me as though I'd never been loved more.

One-way love is always at its most palpable and transformative when we are at our lowest ebb. Grace, like water, flows to the lowest part. "But God demonstrates his own love for us in this: While we were *still sinners*, Christ died for us" (Rom. 5:8 NIV, emphasis mine) is how the apostle Paul puts it. It can be something momentous, like what I just described, or it can be something as mundane as someone giving you a compliment when you're feeling particularly ugly or incompetent.

Second, and perhaps self-explanatory, one-way love comes from outside of us. It is external. We cannot love ourselves in this way, at least not in the midst of real failure. Kim and I could not have assured each other with any confidence. Only a third party could speak such a gracious word and have it be remotely believable. We needed someone who was not in our situation to address it, and not just anyone. We needed someone with authority. My dad.

Third, one-way love is unexpected. Grace is always a surprise. We are hardwired for reciprocity and punishment; tit for tat is an utterly instinctual mode of thinking and living. So when someone withholds judgment, especially when it is deserved, we are astonished. Kim and I were astonished that day, and we still are. When was the last time you were astonished by someone's surprising response of grace toward you?

ANOTHER WAY TO GO

I'll give you another example, this time from literature. One of the most enduring works of art over the past two hundred years is Victor Hugo's *Les Misérables*. Rarely does a decade go by without a fresh film adaptation or staging of the classic musical it inspired. *Les Mis* has stood the test of time for good reason; it is an incredibly moving story of redemption—one that deals with the deepest themes of human life: mercy and guilt, justice and inequality, God and man, men and women, parents and children, forgiveness and punishment, and yes, the relationship of grace and law. It is also a notorious tearjerker. Like a true artist, Hugo burrows inside the rib cage and plays a symphony on our heartstrings. Perhaps it should come as no surprise that the entire story hinges on a stunning act of one-way love.

Out on parole after nineteen years in a French prison, protagonist Jean Valjean is denied shelter at several respectable establishments because his passport identifies him as a former convict. He is finally taken in by a kindly bishop, Bishop Bienvenu. Valjean repays his host by running off in the middle of the night with the church silver. When the police catch up to him, Valjean lies and claims that the bishop gave him the silver as a gift. The police drag him back to the bishop's house, where Bienvenu not only *validates* Valjean's deception but chastises him for not accepting the candlesticks as well.

Jean Valjean is utterly confounded. His identity up until that point had been that of thief, prisoner, number, sinner. Now he has been seen as human and shown mercy.

But it is more than mercy, isn't it? Mercy would involve simply dropping the charges, but the bishop goes further—he actually *rewards* Valjean for his transgression! Bienvenu acts, in other words, in the polar opposite way of what would have been expected of him. He is not wise or responsible. He treats Valjean recklessly, overruling what the law—literally standing in front of him—demands. He takes a major risk and blesses this criminal who has shown no ability to act in a nonshameful way. His love has everything to do with the sacrifice of the one doing the loving rather than the merit of the beloved. Needless to say, when I first saw the scene portrayed on the screen, I fell to pieces.

This one surprising act throws Valjean into a complete breakdown, causing him to question absolutely everything in his life and

the world. In the musical, his bewilderment at the goodness that has
been shown him is made plain when he sings:

> One word from him, and I'd be back
> beneath the lash, upon the rack.
> Instead he offers me my freedom.
> I feel my shame inside me like a knife.
> He told me that I have a soul …
>
> Is there another way to go?[1]

There *is* another way to go, thanks be to God—the way of
grace as opposed to law. It is this way that Valjean takes from this
moment forward—or I should say, the way that takes him. He
doesn't become a superhuman or even any less of a broken vessel,
but from here on out, his life is fueled more by gratitude than
greed, giving than receiving, love than fear. This one moment of
grace changes him in a way that a lifetime of punishment never
could. In fact, Valjean's heroic, self-sacrificing actions in the rest
of the novel flow directly from the word he hears from the bishop,
which is the word of Grace.

Just as it is difficult to experience forgiveness without some
knowledge of what you have done wrong, so it is difficult to understand Grace apart from the Law. If the Law is the first word, Grace
is the last. Listen closely: The Law exposes Valjean (and us), while
Grace exonerates him. The Law diagnoses, but Grace delivers. The
Law accuses, Grace acquits. The Law condemns the best of us,
while Grace saves the worst of us. The Law says "cursed," Grace

says "blessed." The Law says "slave," Grace says "son." The Law says "guilty," Grace says "forgiven." The Law can break a hard heart, but only Grace can heal one. Which is precisely what happens to Valjean. He may be a fictional character, but our response to his predicament is not fictional. The tears come, because each one of us is dying to be treated this way. The scene gets us in touch with that one time someone showed us a little sympathy when we deserved reproach. It points us, in other words, to the truth at the very heart of the universe—the one-way love God has for sinners.

WHAT MAKES A DISCIPLE?

Of course, the one-way love of God is not just something we find in our families or in works of literature. It is the driving theme of the Bible itself. Nowhere is this more striking than in Jesus's dealing with his disciples. His choice of disciples was deeply counterintuitive, almost categorically opposed to any qualifications they might hold for the job. Consider his calling of Levi, also known as Matthew:

> After this he went out and saw a tax collector named Levi, sitting at the tax booth. And he said to him, "Follow me." And leaving everything, he rose and followed him.
>
> And Levi made him a great feast in his house, and there was a large company of tax collectors and others reclining at table with them. And the Pharisees and their scribes grumbled at his disciples, saying,

"Why do you eat and drink with tax collectors and
sinners?" And Jesus answered them, "Those who are
well have no need of a physician, but those who are
sick. I have not come to call the righteous but sinners
to repentance." (Luke 5:27–32)

Jesus was turning the tables on all that we think is good. Tax
collectors were not a respectable lot. They were traitors and villains,
the ancient equivalent of mob loan sharks, extorting their fellow
men for the sake of the occupying Roman government (and their
own pockets). They were widely despised and for good reason. Think
Sheriff of Nottingham in the legend of Robin Hood.

But here we have Jesus interrupting Levi at the office and giving him an invitation to follow. In response, Levi throws a party
(of course!)—not a holy huddle of all the righteous people in town,
but a gathering of fellow scoundrels at his house. The Pharisees
and the scribes naturally object, as do you and I when something
so egregiously irrational happens before our eyes. "Why do you
eat and drink with tax collectors and sinners?" they ask. How does
Jesus answer? With his mission statement: "Those who are well [or
who think they are, like you guys] have no need of a physician
[which is what I am], but those who are sick [like these guys]. I have
not come to call the righteous [like you think you are] but sinners
[like they know they are] to repentance." Jesus didn't just say such
things—he put his money where his mouth was: not one of the
original twelve disciples was a religious person. Christ was interested in those who couldn't bring anything to the table, not those
who thought they could handle this righteousness gig pretty well

on their own. He knew that only those who didn't have anything going for them would be able to accept the one-way transaction. You only go to the doctor when you suspect you're sick.

This is important. As Paul Zahl writes, "One-way love is inscrutable or irrational not only because it is out of relation with the intrinsic circumstances on the part of the receiver. One-way love is also irrational because it reaches out to the specifically undeserving person. This is the beating heart of it."[2] The Gospel is addressed not to the godly but the ungodly (Rom. 5:6), not just those who are down on their luck or brokenhearted and suffering, but to perpetrators themselves—tax collectors, prostitutes, murderers, adulterers. Not just theoretical sinners, but actual flesh-and-blood repeat offenders like me. We celebrate this aspect of one-way love when it is directed our way, but like the Pharisees, we hate it when it is directed at our enemies.

No one in the Bible is more of a repeat offender than the apostle Peter, the so-called "rock" upon which the church is built. His consistent ineptitude is almost comic, or at least it would be, were he not also the one who Jesus appointed to be their chief representative. As you may remember from Sunday school, Jesus called Simon Peter (and his brother Andrew) while they were fishing by the Sea of Galilee. He immediately left his family business and followed the Lord. After he answered Jesus's famous question, "Who do you say that I am?" correctly, Jesus changed his name from Simon to Peter, which means *rock*. Peter lived with Jesus for three and a half years, witnessed many miracles, and heard his teaching. He was part of Jesus's inner circle of three (Peter, James, and John) and was clearly captivated by the Lord and his teaching. Peter was the one who asked

Jesus to explain parables, the one who asked for more clarification about forgiveness. He had given up everything for the Lord he deeply loved (see Matt. 19:27), and he loved his Savior more than he had ever loved anyone.

And yet, his track record was abysmal. A few bullet points from his spiritual resume:

- When Jesus told him to walk on water, Peter was afraid and sank. (Matt. 14:22–33)
- Peter tried to persuade Jesus that he would not have to die and received the following reply: "Get behind me, Satan! You are a stumbling block to me; you do not have in mind the concerns of God but merely human concerns." (Matt. 16:23 NIV)
- He fell asleep in Gethsemane three times, despite the explicit instructions of his sorrowful Lord, who asked him, "Could you not watch one hour?" (Mark 14:32–42)
- When the guards came to arrest Jesus in Gethsemane, Peter drew his sword and Jesus rebuked him for it. (John 18:11)
- After Jesus was arrested, Peter denied him three times, after being told by Jesus—in no uncertain terms—that he was going to do so. (Mark 14:26–31, 66–72)
- When he and John got word that Jesus had risen, they both ran to the empty tomb. It was a race Peter lost. (John 20:4)

Apart from his being the first to acknowledge that Jesus was the Christ, the son of God, almost everything he did in the Gospels ended in a correction, a rebuke, or just simple failure. It is hard to imagine how to be a worse disciple than Peter, short of rejecting the faith entirely, once and for all. He could be relied upon to *fail* at doing God's bidding, with one or two salient exceptions. Yet these exceptions were enough for Jesus to proclaim that he was the rock. Why?

It is no coincidence that Peter was both the weakest and the one who recognized who Jesus was. He could recognize the Savior, because he knew how much he needed one. His faith was directly tied to his failure. As Richard Rohr once wrote, "The great and merciful surprise is that we come to God not by doing it right but by doing it wrong!"[3]

BREAKFAST ON THE BEACH

It gets better though. After the resurrection, the disciples left Jerusalem to return to Galilee. There, by the Sea of Tiberius, Jesus appeared once again to seven of his fearful disciples, but not in anger, disappointment, or judgment. He came to cook breakfast for them:

> Just as day was breaking, Jesus stood on the shore;
> yet the disciples did not know that it was Jesus.
> Jesus said to them, "Children, do you have any
> fish?" (John 21:4–5)

Consider how the Author of one-way love addressed his unbelieving disciples, those who deserted him during his greatest time of need, those who struggled to believe he had risen from the dead. He called them his "children." This word can, of course, be used for one's biological children, but it was also used for "a person of any age for whom there is a special relationship of endearment."[4] He called them his *dear children*.

Jesus then asked them whether they had caught any fish during their night of labor, although he already knew they hadn't. "Cast the net on the right side of the boat, and you will find some," he said. The understatement is astounding. You can almost see him smiling to himself, knowing that they won't just find some, they will be so overwhelmed with fish that their nets may break. Given their dismal performance in Jerusalem, the disciples had every reason to expect punishment, but Jesus had other plans. He knew they were hungry after fishing all night, so he had a charcoal fire ready with food cooking on it. He cared about their hunger, their need.

If you believe that Jesus loves and blesses only "good people," those who stand faithfully in times of trial, never deny him, and always trust and obey, then you'll have a hard time explaining Jesus the short-order cook. If we believe in tit for tat, then what these men had earned was to be shunned and shamed. Where were they when Jesus was in need? When he was hungry and thirsty? When he was in agony? Instead of leaving these turncoats to themselves and finding others who would be more faithful, he gave them yet another gift—not just the disciples in general, but Peter specifically:

> When they had finished breakfast, Jesus said to
> Simon Peter, "Simon, son of John, do you love me
> more than these?" He said to him, "Yes, Lord; you

know that I love you." He said to him, "Feed my lambs." He said to him a second time, "Simon, son of John, do you love me?" He said to him, "Yes, Lord; you know that I love you." He said to him, "Tend my sheep." He said to him the third time, "Simon, son of John, do you love me?" Peter was grieved because he said to him the third time, "Do you love me?" and he said to him, "Lord, you know everything; you know that I love you." Jesus said to him, "Feed my sheep." (John 21:15–17)

Again, consider the scene: Peter's stomach was full. His Lord, whom he loved, had returned, yet the awkwardness of Peter's failures hung in the air. Jesus took him aside for a private stroll down the beach (see John 21:20). Maybe he walked off with him so Peter wouldn't be humiliated in front of the others, who knows? But their conversation was one for the ages.

Three times during this interaction, Jesus addressed Peter as Simon, his "old" name (Matt. 16:14–18). It was in the context of Peter's proclamation of Christ's identity that Jesus gave him his new name. Jesus called him by that old name, Simon, to remind him of his identity outside of Christ: Simon the Poor, Simon the Fisherman, Simon the Loser, Simon the Coward. The word *Simon*, in this sense, is a word of Law.

Jesus asked Simon if he loved him, not once, but three times—the same number of times that Peter had denied him, a coincidence that was clearly not lost on Peter. He realized that the Lord saw him as he was, and whatever sham facade he had been parading in those intervening weeks and months was shattered. Jesus knew Peter's heart better than Peter did himself.

Once Peter was completely dressed down, instead of stripping him of his "post," Jesus did the opposite: he gave him *more* responsibility. Peter had been spectacularly unreliable, and yet Jesus reinstated him as "rock." Irrational, inscrutable, the opposite of a good idea—this is how Christ chooses to work in the world. The wonderful truth is that Jesus doesn't need perfect vessels to accomplish his will. He needs broken ones—men and women who have been slain, humiliated, disillusioned of all their "I can do it, really I can!," "This time I'll try harder!," "Just give me a little more time and some secret steps, and I'll get it together!" self-deception.

Peter was an utter failure on every level, but Jesus commissioned and used him anyway. Why? Because the success of the church doesn't rest on Peter's good—albeit deluded—confessions. It does not rest on us, on our collective abilities or progress *at all*.

The feeding and tending of Christ's flock wasn't contingent upon Peter's abilities, his track record, or even his love for Christ. Jesus didn't need Peter any more than God needed Jonah. Christ's overflowing love restores Peter *for Peter's sake*. He met Peter's failure head-on, in the full light of a morning by the shore, restored him, and commissioned him three times. Remember: Jesus is the one doing the feeding here, not Peter. Did he spend the night fishing? Sure. But how did that work out? They'd caught nothing! So Jesus built a fire and directed fish into their nets and fed them. Then he told Simon, "Feed my sheep." How could he do that? Only because Jesus already had all the feeding that needed to be done well in hand.

Right on the heels of Peter's most disqualifying behavior, Jesus commissioned him. Human wisdom—the wisdom of this world—has no system or plan for dealing with the mistakes of yesterday. What does the wisdom of this world have to say to you and me in the darkness of night, when we are feeling overwhelmed and guilty about yesterday's failures? When we have done the one thing we told ourselves we would never do? Sure, it can assure us that we're not so bad, that these failures are not our fault, but the world's hollow assurances do nothing to assuage the knowledge of our utter failure to palliate our guilt and shame. All the world can do is hand us over to the assaults of conscience or, when our conscience has been so repeatedly bruised and seared, to the dreary deadness and dullness of living life detached from hope. I know firsthand what the world has to offer us in terms of yesterday's failures and the guilt we own: get drunk, fall in love with yourself, buy more things, work harder, tell yourself you're really okay after all.

TOO GOOD TO (NOT) BE TRUE

The one-way love of God meets us in our failures. Our failures make His one-way love that much more glorious. What qualifies us for service is God's devotion to us—not our devotion to Him. This is as plainly as I can say it: the value of our lives rests on God's infinite, incomprehensible, unconditional love for us—not our love for Him. Such relief! We can finally exhale!

When Kim and I took such a right turn all those years ago, and I embraced the faith I had so publicly walked away from, I remember being asked, "What was it about God that was finally so attractive to you? That drew you back to Him?" The answer is a simple yet radical one: God had given me so much—a loving family, a remarkable heritage. I had squandered it all, and He had continued to come after me. His forbearance and His kindness, in the midst of my open rebellion, was just too magnetic in the long haul. It is, after all, the kindness of the Lord that leads to repentance (Rom. 2:4). I didn't deserve it then, and I don't deserve it now.

But wait. Does this mean our failures are somehow victories? That Peter's weakness was a good thing? That my scandalous behavior was any less shortsighted, wrong, or hurtful? No!

This is an extremely important point. The one-way love of God is restorative and reconciling because in the mystery of His cross, God has neutralized the effects of sin, forgiven its offense, blotted out its stain, expiated its guilt, and created a new beginning. "As far as the east is from the west, so far does he remove our transgressions from us" (Ps. 103:12). Thanks to Jesus's sacrifice on my behalf, the sins I cannot forget, God cannot remember. Jesus is not waving some magic wand or being dishonest about who Peter was (or who we are). He is acting on the firm foundation of what his death on our behalf has accomplished. There is nothing cheap about the grace he offers repeat offenders. On the contrary—it cost him everything!

The Gospel announces that Jesus came to acquit the guilty. He came to judge and be judged in our place. Christ came to satisfy the deep judgment against us once and for all so we could be free from the judgment of God, others, and ourselves. Jesus came to unburden us of our efforts at trying to deal with judgment on our own.

In his letter to the Colossians, the apostle Paul announces, "And you, who were dead in your trespasses and the uncircumcision of your flesh, God made alive together with him, having forgiven us all our trespasses, by canceling the record of debt that stood against us with its legal demands. This he set aside, nailing it to the cross" (Col. 2:13–14).

The Gospel declares that our guilt has been atoned for, the Law has been fulfilled. In Christ, the ultimate demand has been met, the deepest judgment has been satisfied. Jesus took on himself all the judgment we deserve from God, so we can be free from the paralyzing fear of judgment. There are no ifs, ands, or buts. We no longer need to live under the burden of trying to appease the judgment we feel, full stop.

In fact, the judgment we feel is just that: a feeling—no longer a reality. We may judge others, and they may judge us; we may judge ourselves, but God does not. His love is one-way, and it is inexhaustible. This is not just good news, this is the *best* news: the assurance that in our darkest moments, when you and I, as a last resort, come knocking on "heaven's door," the voice that greets us is the same one that met Jean Valjean that fateful night:

> You are suffering; you are hungry and thirsty; you
> are welcome. And don't thank me; don't tell me that
> I am taking you into my house. This is the home
> of no man, except the one who needs a refuge. I
> tell you, a traveler, you are more at home here than
> I; whatever is here is yours. Why would I have to
> know your name?… Your name is my brother.[5]

CHAPTER 6

THE UNEXPECTED BENEFITS OF HUGGING A CACTUS

Hollywood is not known as a culture of grace. Dog-eat-dog is more like it. People love you one day and hate you the next. Personal value is attached to box-office revenues and the unpredictable and often cruel winds of fashion. It was doubly shocking, then, when one-way love—and its fruit—made a powerful appearance on the big stage in 2011. The occasion for it was Robert Downey Jr. receiving the American Cinematheque Award, a prize given to an extraordinary artist in the entertainment industry who is "making a significant contribution to the art of the Moving Picture." A big deal, in other words. Downey was allowed to choose who would present him with the award, and he made a bold decision. He selected his one-time costar Mel Gibson to do the honors.

To say that Gibson's reputation had taken a serious nosedive would be a severe understatement. An arrest for drunk driving in 2006, during which the actor-director spewed racist and anti-Semitic epithets, was followed by public infidelity and a high-profile divorce in 2009, and then culminated in 2010 when tapes of a drunk Gibson berating his then-girlfriend in the foulest manner imaginable were released online. *Reprehensible* does not even begin to describe it.

Downey's ceremony took place a little more than a year after that final incident, the one that rightly cemented Gibson's place as pariah *numero uno* in Tinseltown.

Of course, Downey was no stranger to being ostracized. In the 1990s, he became something of punch line himself as someone notoriously unable to kick an addiction to drugs and alcohol. Arrest after arrest, relapse after relapse, people both in Hollywood and elsewhere began to think of him less as an actor and more as a junkie. Professionally, he became a liability—even those who wanted to work with him couldn't because insurance companies wouldn't underwrite a film if he were part of the cast. Bit by bit, and with the notable help of some good friends, Downey eventually got sober, and his career slowly got back on track. In 2008, he was cast as Iron Man, and the rest—as they say—is history. Today he is one of the most beloved and highest grossing actors in the business. So the award coincided with the very height of his popularity and the nadir of Gibson's. This was Downey's moment of glory.

Instead of using his acceptance speech to give an aw-shucks speech to the crowd of adoring colleagues and to doff his hat to his agent and family, Downey did something unprecedented. We'll let him speak for himself:

> Actually, I asked Mel to present this award to me for a reason, because when I couldn't get sober, he told me not to give up hope, and he urged me to find my faith—didn't have to be his or anyone else's as long as it was rooted in forgiveness. And I couldn't get hired, so he cast me in the lead of a movie that was actually developed for him. And he kept a roof over my head, and he kept food on the table. And most importantly, he said that if I accepted responsibility for my wrongdoings, and if I embraced that part of my soul that was ugly—"hugging the cactus" he calls it—he said that if I "hugged the cactus" long enough, I'd become a man of some humility and that my life would take on new meaning. And I did, and it worked. All he asked in return was that someday I help the next guy in some small way. It's reasonable to assume that at the time he didn't imagine the next guy would be him. Or that someday was tonight.
>
> So anyway, on this special occasion … I humbly ask that you join me—unless you are completely without sin (in which case you picked the wrong … industry)—in forgiving my friend his trespasses, offering him the same clean slate you have me, and allowing him to continue his great and ongoing

contribution to our collective art without shame. He's
hugged the cactus long enough. [And then they hug.][1]

The short speech not only testifies to the amazing power of one-
way love; it is itself a beautiful example of the fruit of one-way love.
At his lowest point, Downey was shown mercy by Mel Gibson. He
didn't deserve it—his track record was abysmal—but Gibson, for
whatever reason, took a risk at great cost to himself. He personally
paid the massive insurance premium for Downey on 2003's *The
Singing Detective* so his friend could get back on his feet. You don't
forget something like that.

Downey's response was one of gratitude and generosity. His
speech may have phrased things in terms of repayment, but Gibson's
injunction was obviously an after-the-fact suggestion rather than a
condition. Downey's gesture goes so far beyond any sense of owing,
especially considering the choice of moment and venue. To associate with Gibson in such a public manner, indeed to advocate for
him, meant putting Downey's own reputation on the line. It was a
self-sacrificial and even reckless move. There was no possible gain
for Downey, such was the antipathy that Gibson inspired. No, his
defense of the indefensible was the uncoerced act of a heart that
had been touched by one-way love. There is a direct line from the
love Downey was shown to the love he then showed. His supreme
generosity was the fruit of grace.

Gibson clearly had no idea about what Downey was planning
to do. And Downey's tone and demeanor made it very clear that he
was not putting himself out there under duress—he did it because he
wanted to. His ability and desire to show mercy seem almost directly

proportional to his personal experience of it, his firsthand knowledge that he was just as much in need of mercy as the chief of sinners. His plea, in other words, was rooted in humility about his own sin and gratitude for the love he had been shown, which asserted itself in kind. Belovedness birthed love. Grace accomplished what no amount of court-ordered, legal remedies ever could: it created a heart that desired to show mercy to the "least of these."

Of course, as powerful a story as it is, the episode is not a one-to-one analogy for the Gospel—no story could be. As impressive as Iron Man is, he is not God. But that doesn't mean it isn't close. Thankfully, when it comes to God's Grace, there is not even a hint of exchange. No suggestion of payback or pay-it-forward. There are no strings attached. While only grace can change a heart and produce Law-fulfilling works of mercy, grace is not *dependent* on a changed heart or Law-fulfilling works of mercy. Grace alone produces the conditions that induce change, but grace is not conditional on change. It is pure gift—independent of outcomes. We must be careful here about turning grace into a strategy (or law)—a means by which we can get certain things, control certain things, guarantee certain things. But more on that later.

THE WEE LITTLE MAN

If you grew up going to Sunday school like I did, you are probably familiar with the Wee Little Man named Zacchaeus. Perhaps the name conjures up picture Bibles and coloring books and slightly irritating sing-alongs. Fortunately, no amount of sterilization can obscure what has to be one of the most jaw-dropping instances of one-way love in the entire Bible. Indeed, the story of Zacchaeus gives us a window not only into Christ's love for sinners but the fruit it can bear in a person's life, not to mention the resistance it often encounters from those who witness it. It is a study in the fruit of grace.

A little context: Zacchaeus was essentially the Bernie Madoff of Jericho. As you may remember, in March 2009, Bernie Madoff pled guilty to eleven federal felonies and admitted to having turned his wealth-management business into a massive Ponzi scheme that defrauded investors of billions of dollars. The amount missing from client accounts, including fabricated gains, was nearly $65 billion. Yes, *billion*. That June, he was sentenced to one hundred and fifty years in prison, the maximum allowed.[2] Thousands of people were swindled out of their life savings and retirement funds. Madoff had lived lavishly on their investments—until the money ran out and the deception was exposed.

To say that in certain communities Madoff remains one of the most hated men in the country would be an understatement. His was a kind of old-fashioned villainy that we seldom see in a post-Freudian world, someone who methodically deceived and stole from those who trusted him. There was nothing accidental about his crimes; they were all very much premeditated. The public revilement was justified.

So it was with Zacchaeus. As the *chief* tax collector, the Jewish establishment would have despised him because he collected taxes for Rome, an act that was considered both traitorous and sinful. Yet as a Jew, he would have been shunned by his imperial employers as well. Even the other tax collectors would have hated him, because he likely cheated them, too, skimming funds off the top of their ill-gotten cash. Add to the mix an inevitable Napoleon complex, and you have a picture of a loathsome loan shark who used his authority to extort his countrymen for both his own personal gain and that of the occupying Roman government. Like Madoff's, his reputation would have been well-founded, which makes Jesus's actions even more surprising:

> [Jesus] entered Jericho and was passing through. And behold, there was a man named Zacchaeus. He was a chief tax collector and was rich. And he was seeking to see who Jesus was, but on account of the crowd he could not, because he was small in stature. So he ran on ahead and climbed up into a sycamore tree to see him, for he was about to pass that way. And when Jesus came to the place, he looked up and said to him, "Zacchaeus, hurry and come down, for I must stay at your house today." So he hurried and came down and received him joyfully. (Luke 19:1–6)

Jesus singled out Zacchaeus, despite the fact that Zacchaeus had not said or done anything to warrant or attract his attention. Zacchaeus simply did what he would for any passing sideshow, namely, climbed a tree, so he could catch a glimpse of what was going on. There was no gesture of repentance, no prayers, no tears, no words! The initiative belonged to Jesus alone. And Jesus didn't say, "I *want* to stay at your house," or "Would you be so kind as to invite me over for tea?" He said, "I *must* stay at your house." The request is less of a request than an imperative.

Imagine if a well-known spiritual leader visited the city where Madoff is incarcerated and, to the astonishment of everyone around, marched right past all the churches and universities, past all the pastors clamoring for him to address their congregations, past all the journalists dying for an interview, past all the autograph seekers and mildly curious, straight to the prison. He then informs the warden that he *must* have lunch with Bernie. It is his number one priority. He's not there to castigate Madoff or pick his brain in a "How could he?" kind of way. He is simply there to have lunch and spend some time with the guy no one wants to touch with a ten-foot pole. How do you think all the honest people would respond? They would be shocked, confused, and probably pretty insulted.

THE RESPONSE

We can safely assume that Zacchaeus would be taken aback that Jesus wanted to spend time with him. You can almost hear his incredulous reply, "You want to come to *my* house? You want to associate with *me*? Are you sure you got the right guy?" That's conjecture, of course, but the broad strokes of his response in the text are remarkable. "So [Zacchaeus] hurried and came down and received him joyfully." Zacchaeus did not hesitate to respond to Jesus—there was no scoffing, no song and dance, just enthusiasm and joy. Christ's entreaty inspires!

We might wonder how long it had been since anyone other than fellow tax collectors and perhaps a few lowlife friends had visited Zacchaeus. Did he actually have any friends or family? He would have had to work hard to become the chief tax collector: he probably would have had to sacrifice more than a few relationships on the altar of ambition. Maybe he had tried to satisfy himself with the luxury and self-indulgence that his riches afforded him, and maybe he had found that rather than satiating his appetite, they only made it worse. Maybe he was both lonely and desperate. Whatever the case, the immediacy and exuberance of his response suggests that no one had to tell Zacchaeus he was lost. He was all too aware of his station.

What happened next is even more shocking. "And Zacchaeus stood and said to the Lord, 'Behold, Lord, the half of my goods I give to the poor. And if I have defrauded anyone of anything, I restore it fourfold'" (Luke 19:8).

The fruit of grace in this instance was spontaneous, borderline absurd generosity. This is what the apostle John meant when he wrote, "We love because he first loved us" (1 John 4:19). He inverts the way we normally think about these things. Jesus approached Zacchaeus before he had the chance to exhibit any receptiveness, let alone sorrow or eagerness. What's more, at no point did Jesus lean in and tell his new friend, "Listen, I don't want to embarrass you in front of everyone, but you and I both know you need to clean up your act. If you want to continue hanging out, you need to make things right, starting with your pocketbook." Zacchaeus's joyful charity was not the preface to God's grace—it was its result.

The truth is, Jesus didn't require anything of Zacchaeus. He didn't force, coerce, or guilt Zacchaeus into giving back what he stole; he just loved him. And yet the natural fruit—and what is fruit if not natural?—of this one-way love turned out to be far more extravagant than anything Christ would have suggested. *Obedience* would be too weak a word to describe Zacchaeus's actions. Nowhere in the Law does it require a person to give half of their goods to the poor. Similarly, repaying someone you have defrauded by a factor of four is far beyond the call of duty. Zacchaeus does *more* than the right thing, and he does it spontaneously, cheerfully, and abundantly.

A grateful heart is a generous heart, and a generous heart is a liberated heart. It is no coincidence that the very thing to which Zacchaeus was most enslaved—money—is the very thing that he was inspired to give away so freely.

This isn't just how things work in the Bible—this is real life! Gratitude is the starting point. In 2011, *The New York Times* published an article claiming that feelings of gratitude have "been linked to better health, sounder sleep, less anxiety and depression, higher long-term satisfaction with life and kinder behavior toward others, including romantic partners." Elsewhere in the article, University of Miami psychologist Dr. Michael McCullough is quoted as saying, "More than other emotion, gratitude is the emotion of friendship."[3] We see glimpses of this dynamic everywhere we go.

I know what you're thinking. If the key to inspiring altruism and moral behavior and general well-being is fostering an "attitude of gratitude," and gratitude is the natural response to the good news of the Gospel, why don't more churches preach grace every week? The common misunderstanding, especially in the church, is that moral compliance comes through responsible instruction and exhortation, that in order to ensure good behavior in our fellow man, we need the law. One of the church's main tasks, therefore, is to tell people what to do. But that's not what we see in the story of Zacchaeus, and that's not what we see in our own lives either.

Christians often speak about grace with a thousand qualifications. They add all sorts of buts and brakes. Listen for them! Our greatest concern, it seems, is that people will take advantage of grace and use it as a justification to live licentiously. Sadly, while attacks on morality typically come from outside the church, attacks on grace typically come from inside the church. The reason is because somewhere along the way, we've come to believe that this whole enterprise is about behavioral modification, and grace just doesn't possess the teeth to scare us into changing, so we end up hearing more about what grace isn't than we do about what grace is. Some would even say that "Yes grace, but ..." originated with the Devil in the Garden of Eden (Gen. 3), that the biggest lie Satan wants the church to believe is that grace is dangerous and therefore needs to be kept in check. Sadly, the church has believed this lie all too well.

Where disobedience flourishes, it is not the fault of too much grace but rather of our failure to grasp the depth of God's one-way love for us in the midst of our transgressions and greed. Grace and obedience are *not* enemies, not by a long shot.

Imagine for a second that your dear little four-year-old daughter has just fallen off her bike and is lying by the road, scraped up, bleeding, hurt, and crying. As a loving parent, you don't stop to ask, "What should I do here? Maybe I should just let her bleed a little more so she learns to ride better," do you? No! You instinctively run to help! You don't think, philosophize, or theologize. You just run. Your feet start moving because you love. That's the way love responds. That's the kind of spontaneous goodness that grace draws from us. *Real Christian growth is like learning to drive: the need for constant instruction should slowly give way to instinct.* This is precisely what we see so remarkably and clearly in the story of Zaccheaus.

NOT EVERYONE IS THRILLED

Zacchaeus's response is not the only one we find in the passage. We also read about the crowd that witnessed the interaction. Luke 19:7 tells us, "And when they saw it, they all grumbled, 'He has gone in to be the guest of a man who is a sinner.'" The crowd was scandalized. They were upset. Jesus had decided to associate himself with the most despised man in the city. The last person he *should* be associating himself with, at least if their conception of what it means to be a holy person had any basis. By doing so, Jesus had become the object of scorn and ridicule himself. The hatred and suspicion that had been focused on Zacchaeus was now leveled at the Lord as well. This is what we commonly call "guilt by association."

It's easy for us to look back on this episode from our comfortable present-day perch and deride the crowd for their self-righteousness, limited vision, and uncharitable spirit. But that is only because we've got the privilege of hindsight. Like Robert Downey Jr.'s speech, this story should violate our deepest beliefs about fairness and justice and reciprocity. Make no mistake: if we had been part of the mob that day, we would have reacted the same way they did. Jesus was consciously disregarding the accepted pecking order—upending the *God-given* scale of righteousness and deserving. The only people who wouldn't have felt threatened by such a move would have been those who didn't understand what he was doing.

The crowd, like us, would have assumed that God cares about the clean and competent. They were operating from the same transactional, conditional mentality that we do, the same system whose motto is that irrepressible but utterly nonbiblical slogan "God helps those who help themselves." (Believe it or not, a survey in 2000 showed that 68 percent of people in the church believe that's a verse in the Bible![4])

This misapprehension is so prevalent because it is the natural instinct of people everywhere who are addicted to their own sense of control, religious or not. It is what we desperately *want* to be true about God—that He is beholden to our hard work and moral effort. Under the spell of a sense of entitlement, we turn the Gospel into just another narcissistic self-help program. We attend and promulgate churches that preach "humanity and it improved" rather than "Christ and him crucified" (1 Cor. 2:2).

The ridiculous way some have taken this story and made into just such a program—Zacchaeus climbed his tree; have you climbed yours?—only proves all the more that, apart from God's work, we hate grace as much as that crowd did.

Fortunately, Jesus made very clear what his mission was. The story ends with him saying, "Today salvation has come to this house, since he also is a son of Abraham. For the Son of Man came to seek and to save the lost" (Luke 19:9–10). I'm not sure how he could make it any plainer! Jesus is not being cavalier about wrongdoing or suggesting that greed, and its fallout, is not a big deal. He shed tears over our sin; he came to suffer and die for it. No, this is Jesus identifying with the sinner and loving those who least deserve it. He knows that the only way to break the cycle of retribution and oppression and heartbreak is to demolish the ladder of deserving altogether.

It is no surprise that this story comes right on the heels of Christ's pronouncement that "it is easier for a camel to go through the eye of a needle than for a rich person to enter the kingdom of God" (Luke 18:25). Zacchaeus was just such a man. But Jesus did not come for the "good people" who need a helping hand. He came for those who are completely hopeless without him! In other words, God doesn't select His team the way the NFL does in the April draft. He isn't looking for the best athletes around, or even those with the most potential. In fact, the apostle Paul said exactly the opposite:

> But God chose what is foolish in the world to
> shame the wise; God chose what is weak in the
> world to shame the strong; God chose what is low
> and despised in the world, even things that are
> not, to bring to nothing things that are, so that no
> human being might boast in the presence of God.
> (1 Cor. 1:27–29)

God lavishes His grace on the foolish, the weak, the despised, and the nothings so He alone will get the glory. What would we think of grace if God pursued the guy who had been voted Most Likely to Succeed in his high school yearbook? Such an endorsement would only affirm the law-driven conditionality that is already firmly entrenched in our hearts. Instead, He pursues those who are not confused about their need, the Zacchaeuses and Bernie Madoffs and Mel Gibsons of the world. Which is profoundly good news to those of us whose lives have been more marked by failure and self-induced ostracizing than by success and belonging.

HONEST AND FREE

One surefire way to know you're starting to grasp this message of grace is when you're finally able to admit that you're not the good guy—that you never were and apart from grace never will be. In other words, when you finally find yourself being honest about who you are. The freedom of the Gospel is the freedom to stop pretending you are anything but a fellow Zacchaeus, a sinner in need of a Savior.

Nowhere in the Bible is this transparency more palpable than with the apostle Paul. This is the man who wrote a significant portion of the New Testament, planted countless churches, suffered intense persecution for the sake of the Gospel, and eventually was imprisoned. If there ever was a supersaint, it was Paul. But that's not how he saw himself. At the end of his life, with acute self-awareness, he said, "Christ Jesus came into the world to save sinners—of whom I am the worst" (1 Tim. 1:15 NIV). Paul was not expressing some pietistic form of self-loathing or false humility; this is what Robert Downey Jr. was alluding to when he talked about "hugging the cactus."

Compassion for others—the desire to serve and sacrifice—flows out of the honest recognition of who we are and God's love for us in the midst of that. As T. S. Eliot wrote in his *Four Quartets*, "The only wisdom we can hope to acquire / Is the wisdom of humility: humility is endless."

Paul was a man who was simply no longer hung up on justifying himself, who could embrace and even celebrate his weaknesses in the knowledge that the Son of Man came to seek and save those who are lost. He had been set free from himself.

There's a great story about an old Lutheran pastor who, on his deathbed, voiced his confidence that he would be received in heaven, because he could not remember having done one truly good work. He meant that he wasn't trusting in any of his works, but rather in Christ and his righteousness alone. That was a man at peace! He did not go to his grave anxious about trying to prove himself. He had given up on that particular endeavor, only to find that there was One who had already done for him what he could not do for himself.

As a side note, when we no longer look to ourselves for salvation, we are free to not take ourselves so seriously! Self-deprecation, the ability to laugh at oneself, is a fruit of the Spirit as far as I'm concerned.

So whereas self-salvation projects, by definition, require us to lie to ourselves and others in order to maintain our narrative of improvement—remaining ever vigilant (and dead serious) about how we are doing and coming across—one-way love engenders the kind of humility that leads to compassion for others who are in similarly bad shape.

In my own life, I've certainly found this to be true: The more I focus on how I am doing—the more I check my spiritual pulse—the more anxious and neurotic I become. The more I obsess over my need to get better, the worse I actually get; I become morbidly introspective and self-absorbed. And because I'm so preoccupied with me—how I'm doing, if I'm growing, whether I'm doing it right or not, spending too much time pondering my spiritual failures and brooding over my spiritual successes—I become less willing and able to notice the needs of others around me and meet those needs.

In fact, you might say that the biggest difference between the practical effect of sin and the practical effect of the Gospel is that sin turns us inward while the Gospel turns us outward, as it did with Zacchaeus. Any version of "the Gospel" or "grace," therefore, that encourages you to think about yourself and your performance will inevitably be co-opted by what Martin Luther called our curved-in nature (*incurvatus in se*)—whether it's your failures or your successes; your good works or your bad works; your strengths or your weaknesses; your obedience or your disobedience. We will explore this at more length in the coming chapter's discussion of self-forgetfulness.

ANY LASTING CHANGE

This entire chapter can be summed up in the following way: Grace inspires what the Law demands. The Law prescribes good works, but only grace can produce them. While the Law directs, the Gospel alone delivers. Gratitude, generosity, honesty, compassion, acts of mercy and self-sacrifice, these things spring unsummoned from a forgiven heart. When Paul Zahl writes that "the one-way love ... is the essence of any lasting transformation that takes place in human experience,"[5] he is 100 percent right.

Think about it for a moment in your own life: beneath your happiest moments and closest relationships inevitably lies some instance of being loved in midst of weakness and/or deserved judgment. It could be something as small as a kind word when you were feeling

particularly vulnerable, or something as significant as a friend publicly advocating for you despite your obvious guilt. But whatever it
was, it made all the difference. These things may not happen every
day—indeed, one-way love is both rare and surprising—but when
they do, they are indelible. We can trace our patience with our children back to those times when our parents were patient with us,
our commitment to our spouses back to a moment of forgiveness,
the likes of which we had never experienced before (or sometimes,
since). Our confidence in our work dates back to the afternoon our
Little League coach decided not to take us out of the game after
we'd made a grievous error. We volunteer at a suicide hotline because
someone once listened to us, really listened to us, when we were
depressed, and it was the beginning of a new lease on life. The list
goes on. Grace bears fruit.

Again, this is not to say grace *requires* an outcome—it is one-way!
It does not speak the language of results or consequences, which is
precisely why such wonderful and exciting things often happen when
it is in the mix. In other words, one-way love cannot be mandated,
thank God; it can only be experienced. My friend Justin Holcomb
tells a story about just such a life-altering instance of grace, one that
changed his life forever:

> My understanding of unconditional love and its
> implications germinated when I was ten years old
> and flooded our next-door neighbor's home. Our
> neighbors had moved and were trying to sell their
> house. One day, I broke in through the back door
> and closed the drains in all of the sinks and tubs

and turned on all the faucets. Then, I just sat and watched water flood the entire house. I let the water run while I went home for dinner, returning a few hours later to turn it off.

I knew what I had done was wrong, and I was even shocked that I had wanted to do something so destructive. When our neighbors found the damage the following day while showing the home to prospective buyers, they came to our house and asked my family if we had seen anyone around their place recently. On top of what I had already done, I lied to my neighbors and my parents.

I felt completely messed up. I was destroying stuff for the sake of destroying and then lying blatantly to everyone. I had heard about asking God's forgiveness (my dad had taught me the Lord's Prayer), so I begged God to forgive. I was worried that He wouldn't. Surely something so deliberate and cruel was just too much to forgive.

After a month with an uneasy conscience, I was finally found out. Another neighbor had seen me sneaking around and told my parents. My father called me in from playing outside with my friends and asked me if I remembered anything important about the flooding incident. I knew something was up, but I felt I had to stick with the lie at this point. Finally, my dad told me that I was busted. I experienced an overwhelming sense of shame and guilt for my sins, as well as an intense fear of the consequences. I sobbed and muttered, "Dad, I'm so sorry. I've been asking God to forgive me for so long, and I don't know if He ever will." In a moment of parental love and great wisdom, my dad said, "If you asked God to forgive you, then you are forgiven. You deserve to be punished, and this will cost a lot of money to fix. But, son, you are forgiven. Go back outside and play."[6]

The fruit of one-way love in Justin's life was not only a renewed love for his father and genuine willingness to behave (for a while, at least!) but a faith in God's mercy and love that has gripped and carried him to this very day. As of this writing, Justin's most recent book is titled *On the Grace of God*.

A FINAL WORD

The grace that Jesus showed Zacchaeus is only a preview of what awaited him at the cross. The cross is where his mission to "seek and save the lost" was ultimately accomplished. Remember, he died a criminal's death. In that fateful moment, Jesus not only associated himself with tax collectors and prostitutes and lepers and movie stars and addicts and preachers and mischievous teenagers, he bore their sin on his shoulders. He bore *our* sin—every last drop. There was nothing partial; it was and it is the apex of one-way love. Jesus suffered the scorn, the punishment, and the wrath we deserve, and in return gives us the gift of his righteousness. It cannot be undone.

Those who are lost are found, and where there was once judgment, there is now only love, extravagant and free. Where there was once guilt by association, now there is only glory by association.

So … that cactus you're so cozy with? You can hug it all you want—the needles have fallen off.

CHAPTER 7

GRACE IN EVERYDAY LIFE

In 2007, the New York–based website Gawker.com named John Fitzgerald Page "The Worst Person in the World."[1] John, a young professional in Atlanta at the time, was awarded the dubious title after an exchange he had with a young woman on Match.com, an online dating site, was made public. The young lady in question had made an overture by "winking" at John, admitting in retrospect that she probably should have thought twice "considering his screen name was 'IvyLeagueAlum.'"

John responded with a short, introductory message, listing several facts about himself, some relevant, some less so (height, weight, schools attended, fitness regimen). He also asked a couple of pointed questions of his new admirer—where she had gone to school, the kind of products she enjoyed, and what activities she currently participated in to stay in shape. He seemed especially concerned that his would-be date was not misrepresenting herself physically. John had apparently been "deceived before by inaccurate representations"—given the circumstances, an honest concern. More problematic was the self-satisfied tone in which his concern was expressed.

Something about his message must have rubbed its recipient the wrong way, as she replied with a perfunctory "No thanks." Presumably the end of the story. But a spurned John shot back:

> I think you forgot how this works. You hit on me, and therefore have to impress ME and pass MY criteria and standards—not vice versa. 6 pictures of just your head and your inability to answer a simple question lets me know one thing. You are not in shape. I am a trainer on the side, in fact, I am heading to the gym in 26 minutes!
>
> So next time you meet a guy of my caliber, instead of trying to turn it around, just get to the gym! I will even give you one free training session, so you don't blow it with the next 8.9 on Hot or Not, Ivy League grad, Mensa member, can bench/squat/leg press over 1200 lbs., has had lunch with the secretary of defense, has an MBA from the top school in the country, drives a Beemer convertible, has been in 14 major motion pictures, was in Jezebel's Best dressed, etc. Oh, that is right, there aren't any more of those!

In the face of rejection, poor John defended himself. In fact, he did more than that; he justified himself. He listed his achievements, his attributes and accolades—some of which are, on the surface, impressive. John's problem isn't his résumé; it's what he *thinks* about his résumé. He used it to justify his existence, leaning on it for righteousness, and therefore, life and love. Yet no one can love a résumé, and not just because we can know a million things about a person and still not know them. No, love that depends on certain standards of performance isn't really love at all. It's more like emotional bartering, a two-way dynamic if ever there was one. It alienates.[2]

We might like to think John is an extreme case, but he's not—at least not as much as we might wish he were. Maybe there is someone in your life who makes you feel insecure; someone whose very existence you find to be threatening—a walking judgment, if you will. Maybe you find yourself dropping names around that person, talking about things you think might impress them. We may not (hopefully) be as brazen or impulsive as John Fitzgerald Page in flaunting our advantages or achievements, but all of us are performancists in some arena, wired for control and proving.

The truth is, narratives of self-justification burble beneath more of our relationships and endeavors than we would care to admit. In fact, the need to justify ourselves drives an enormous amount of daily life, especially the exhausting parts. This chapter seeks to lay out some of the specific implications one-way love might have in the lives of self-justifying men and women, especially in how we relate to our spouses, our children, and ourselves.

GRACE AND PERSONAL IDENTITY

Starting at the back of the line, the area of personal identity is a place where the rubber of grace meets the road of everyday life in an especially palpable way. If an identity based on "works of the law" looks like John Fitzgerald Page, what might one based in the one-way love of God? For an answer, we need look no further than the apostle Paul, who once wrote a letter not too dissimilar from that of John Fitzgerald Page:

> If anyone else thinks he has reason for confidence in the flesh, I have more: circumcised on the eighth day, of the people of Israel, of the tribe of Benjamin, a Hebrew of Hebrews; as to the law, a Pharisee; as to zeal, a persecutor of the church; as to righteousness under the law, blameless. (Phil. 3:4–6)

Paul, it would seem, had plenty to be proud of. His pedigree, his track record, his religious standing were all impeccable. If he had wanted to justify his existence, he would have had a comparably solid basis on which to do so—the first-century Jewish equivalent of blue blood, Ivy League, Fortune 500 status. But unlike John Fitzgerald Page, Paul doesn't end there. Or you might say, that's *exactly* where he ends:

> But whatever gain I had, I counted as loss for the sake of Christ. Indeed, I count everything as loss

> because of the surpassing worth of knowing Christ
> Jesus my Lord. For his sake I have suffered the loss
> of all things and count them as rubbish, in order
> that I may gain Christ and be found in him, not
> having a righteousness of my own that comes from
> the law, but that which comes through faith in
> Christ, the righteousness from God that depends
> on faith. (Phil. 3:7–9)

The contrast Paul makes here is between a "righteousness of my own that comes from the law" and "the righteousness from God that depends on faith [in Christ]." One is earned, and the other is bestowed, or you might say one is a paycheck while the other is a gift. One is based on our own efforts and attributes; the other is based on God's. One has to do with getting, the other with receiving; one with action, the other with faith. The funny thing is that while the latter is so clearly preferable to the former, we almost always choose the wrong one!

Paul's identity is anchored in Christ's accomplishment, not his own; Christ's strength, not his; Christ's pedigree and track record, not his own; Christ's victory, not Paul's. What a relief. If Paul, whose accomplishments are not exactly small potatoes, saw this as something so good that he was willing to suffer "the loss of all things," then how much sweeter for those of us who didn't start umpteen churches or write a sizeable chunk of the New Testament! Achievements, reputations, strengths, weaknesses, family backgrounds, education, looks, and so on—these things still exist, of course, but only for their own sake. They are divested of the weight they were never meant to bear in the first place, and as such, they can be enjoyed or appreciated without being worshipped. In fact, Paul counts them as loss, which is perhaps a little ironic, since most of the things we tend to define ourselves by are things we're going to lose anyway, if not through aging (beauty, strength, smarts, etc.), then through death (name, wealth, regard).

An identity based in the one-way love of God does not take into account public opinion or, thankfully, even personal opinion. It is a gift from Someone who is not you. As my friend Justin Buzzard wrote recently, "The gospel doesn't just free you from what other people think about you, it frees you from what you think about yourself."[3] In other words, you are not who others see you to be, and you are not who you see yourself to be; you are who God sees you to be—His beloved child, with whom He is well pleased.

I'll say it again, because I need to hear it as much as anyone: the one-way love of God frees us from the oppressive pressure to perform, the slavish demand to "become." God is not waiting for us to do or not do something in order to unlock His love. The Gospel declares that in Christ, we already are everything we need to be. His righteousness has been imputed to us, just as our sin was imputed to him, and as a result we are "found in him." Actually, Paul goes even further than that. He speaks of our "having been buried with [Christ] in baptism, in which [we] were also raised *with him* through faith in the powerful working of God, who raised him from the dead" (Col. 2:12, emphasis mine). Our old identity—the things that previously "made us"—has been put to death. Our new identity is "in Christ."

We have been given a worth and purpose and security and significance, next to which the things of this world are revealed to be transitory at best. What more could we possibly want or need?

SELF-FORGETFULNESS

We are talking here about freedom from self, what Tim Keller calls "the freedom of self-forgetfulness." Preoccupation with our performance actually hinders our performance, does it not? Constant introspection makes us increasingly self-centered—the exact opposite of how the Bible describes obedience or goodness. We might even say that, in one sense, sanctification is the process of forgetting about ourselves. "He must increase, but I must decrease" (John 3:30). Decreasing is impossible for the person who keeps thinking about himself. C. S. Lewis said that we'll know a truly humble man when we meet him because "he will not be thinking about humility: he will not be thinking about himself at all."[4] When we spend more time thinking about ourselves and how we're doing than we do about Jesus and what he's done, we shrink into ourselves. As any gardener will tell you, no seed can grow if it is constantly being dug up to check on its progress.

To be clear, we are not talking about self-loathing or false humility. The opposite! One-way love frees us from the burden of having to establish our own worth, which means we can actually enjoy and appreciate the gifts God has given us on their own terms rather than as means to an end, condemning ourselves for not being good enough stewards. German theologian Oswald Bayer makes the important point that, far from being a "deadening of self," forgetting yourself leads to life and freedom:

> Those who are born anew are no longer entangled
> with themselves. They are solidly freed from this

entanglement, from the self-reflection that always
seeks what belongs to itself. This is not a deadening
of self. It does not flee from thought and responsibility. No, it is the gift of self-forgetfulness. The
passive righteousness of faith tells us: You do not
concern yourself at all! In that God does what is
decisive in us, we may live outside ourselves and
solely in him. Thus, we are hidden from ourselves,
and removed from the judgment of others or the
judgment of ourselves about ourselves as a final
judgment. "Who am I?" Such self-reflection never
finds peace in itself.[5]

Make no mistake, as long as we're living in this world, we will
be tempted to locate our identity in something or someone smaller
than Jesus. Not just tempted, we *will* locate our identity in all sorts
of things that will disappoint us. That is what it means to be addicted
to control, after all. We will listen to the words we read on billboards
and hear on TV, the voices inside our own heads that tell us we are not
enough, that we have to go out and "get it," that it is up to us to secure
our significance, legacy, and impact. We may even find ourselves writing emails that sound like John Fitzgerald Page's. Fortunately, the gift
of identity we have been given in Christ is not contingent upon our
grasping it tightly enough, either spiritually or intellectually. If it were,
it wouldn't be much of a gift! It is contingent only on Christ's dying
and rising again. It persists even when we resist.

The Gospel, in other words, liberates us to be okay with not
being okay. We can stop pretending that we are anyone but who we

actually are. Which means we can admit our weaknesses to ourselves without feeling as if the flesh is being ripped off our bones. We can take off our masks and explore our self-justifying compulsions from a safe distance.

When you understand that your significance, security, and identity are all locked in Christ, you don't have to win—you're free to lose. And nothing in this broken world can beat a person who isn't afraid to lose! You may even find you're free enough to say crazy, risky, counterintuitive stuff like, "To live is Christ and to die is gain"!

GRACE IN RELATIONSHIPS

As we discussed in chapter 3, every relationship, to some degree or another, is assaulted by an aroma of judgment—the sense that we will never measure up to the expectations and demands of another. Critical environments are contexts that, while never explicitly stated, shout: "My approval of you, love for you, and joy in you depends on your ability to measure up to my standards, to become what I need you to become in order for me to be happy." It's a context in which achievement precedes acceptance. We've all felt this. We've felt it at school, in churches, in the workplace, with our friends, a boyfriend, a girlfriend, and most painfully, at home with our spouses, our children, our siblings, and our parents. This is why any relationship where criticism is constant, where you always feel like you're being evaluated and falling short, is an unhappy relationship. Relational demand always creates relational detachment.

The funny thing is that while such situations often seem to be dominated by law, it's usually the cheap kind. That is to say, as we noted before, hypercritical and oppressively legalistic environments are not dominated *enough* by law! They run on an inflated view of human nature, the idea that, through hard work and determination, we can meet whatever standard has been set. And so we become demanding of ourselves. We become our own personal taskmasters, perfectionistic and inflexible. "Just do it" becomes our mantra. And when we finally realize we can't measure up, what happens? Maybe we despair and withdraw, or maybe we start pretending to be someone capable of meeting whatever standard we've fallen short of: "I hope people don't find out who I really am, because I am a train wreck. I am not pulling this off. I'm not getting it done. I may have achieved a great level of success in business, but my kids can't stand me. My wife is just going along for the ride, because she needs me to support her, but she doesn't want to be around me. I'm lonely. I have no friends. I've lived my life for the wrong things and for the wrong reasons." A high view of human nature can turn life into a friendless masquerade in pursuit of self-acceptance. A graceless existence, in other words.

This extends to our relationships with other people as well. "If I can't do it, you had better do it for me." "If I can't get it done, you have to get it done for me." Parents frequently do this with their children. They try to live vicariously through them, because they're disappointed in themselves. They hope their children will become everything they've failed to be, and as any child knows, that is a terrible burden to put on the shoulders of a kid. "I can't be happy unless you do well. You have to become the best that you can be, so I can feel like I'm okay."

Again, the burden we place on one another's shoulders to be our messiah is the result of having a low view of the law—a we-can-do-it approach to life. If our foundational presupposition is that we can keep the law, then when we fail, we will look around for someone to keep it for us, to be our functional saviors. We will look to our spouses or kids or coworkers and say, "I can't do this, but you'd better! If you can perform for me, life might be worth living, and I can silence the siren cries of all my faults and failures."

In case you can't tell, I am convinced that a low view of the law and our need for grace is the number one cause of relational breakdown. You don't have to be a marriage therapist to see that some form of codependency—where one partner feels like the overbearing parent and the other like the irresponsible child—lies at the root of almost all marital strife. We demand that our spouses perform and provide for us—or our spouses demand that of us. "You must save me. I need you to fulfill my unmet needs, because I can't." We use one another in the basest and most selfish ways: for our own self-aggrandizement.

One resounding principle here is that expectation is the mother of resentment. When our spouses or friends have failed to meet our expectations, the little-l laws we have set for them with or without their knowledge, we get angry and we blame. The book of James tells us what causes quarrels and fights among us. Ten times out of ten it is our desires, our misguided craving for self-approval. "Is it not this, that your passions are at war within you? You desire and do not have, so you murder" (James 4:1–2). That's right, *murder*—perhaps not with guns or knives, but in our thoughts and with our words. We execute one another in our hearts.

I remember a psychologist telling me once that there is always hope for a couple that is actively fighting. It's once they stop, once the hurt turns into contempt, when they have effectively killed each other, that the end is nigh.

And yet we foolishly clamor for more and more rules, creating escalating expectations of each other. James goes on to say, "You covet and cannot obtain, so you fight and quarrel" (James 4:2). We look at the accolades others receive, and we think they should be ours, too, so we fight and quarrel and expect more and more. We all expect others to keep the law (little l or big), even though we don't. If we had a more realistic view of ourselves, we might find that we had more compassion for our fellow sufferers, but alas, the judgment seat is too comfortable.

Our anger and gracelessness toward other people is rooted in the fact that we are depending on them to provide for us what we cannot provide for ourselves: righteousness, all-right-ness, forgiveness, freedom from guilt, and freedom from the nagging feeling that we're really not okay (later on we will hear about one such marriage and how it was saved).

People let us down because they can't give us what we want, and we continue to believe that they should. *For crying out loud!* we think. *Somebody should be able to keep the law for me and make me okay!*

We've forgotten that Someone already has.

A SHORT DISCLAIMER

The Gospel heralds a great reversal in which acceptance precedes achievement and mercy comes before merit. It may be rare, but we occasionally see this vertical dynamic playing out in inspiring ways in our horizontal relationships. Look closely at the relationships you find most sustaining and least exhausting, and you will inevitably find some element of unconditionality. Look at the transformative experiences with other people, and you will likely find it there, too. As we said in the last chapter, one-way love lies at the root of all positive and lasting transformations in human behavior. When was the last time you watched someone fall in love? There's always an ugly-duckling-becoming-a-swan aspect to it. A person who is loved in their weakness blossoms. Soon they are exhibiting traits we have never seen before, walking with a newfound confidence; they may even start to look different. It's miraculous.

The trick here, as we mentioned earlier, is that love like this can never be mandated. It has to come from the heart. Recently, I asked my daughter, Genna, about this while we were in the car together. I said, "Genna, have you ever been truly grateful simply because Mom or Dad told you to be grateful?"

Genna hesitated before she answered, probably wondering if she would get in trouble for being honest. Finally she said, "No."

I then said, "Let's say we get in the car after dinner, and I say to you, 'Genna, did Daddy buy your dinner?' and you respond, 'Yes,' and then I prompt you, 'Why don't you say thank you?' Does that make you grateful at all?"

"No."

So she says thank you to me not because she's grateful, but because she wants to comply or because she doesn't want to feel guilty or get in trouble. Isn't that how it is for all of us? Unless our gratitude is inspired by an experience of love, it's not the kind of gratitude that God—or anyone else, really—is interested in. The moment we try to leverage it is the moment it is squashed.

As we noted before, the law-addled human heart tends to take descriptions of grace in practice and fashion them into new, stronger tools that will finally change those we would like to change (in the ways we deem fit). Demand has failed to produce the desired effect, so now we'll try "grace." But just because we can't summon it on our own strength does not mean it doesn't exist. It does! In fact, as Princess Leia said of Obi-Wan Kenobi, grace is "our only hope" for healthy and/or restored relationships.

Again, real grace is impervious to manipulation. As soon as it becomes attached to an intended consequence (a condition), it is no longer one-way, no longer grace. Grace loves without reference to what may or may not happen—which is precisely why such incredible things do happen! Meaning, one-way love *is* the answer to whatever relational strife you're experiencing at the moment, but as soon as it's employed as a fix, it is no longer one-way. It is paradoxical in this respect. The theological way to express this truth is that the command to love is the Law, but the experience of belovedness is the Gospel. This doesn't mean that *trying* to be loving or gracious with another person is ever a bad thing—of course not! It's certainly better than being malicious, and to say otherwise would be to make a contract with despair. But when we find loving another person to be utterly impossible, we can rest in the knowledge that when transforming love comes, it will flow without coercion from a grateful heart, not because of an exertion of our willpower. In fact, the human condition being what it is, one-way love more often than not flows in spite of the exertion of willpower.

So I can describe what one-way love looks like in relationships, I can give you plenty of examples, but I unfortunately can't give you any how-tos (except to pray). All I can say is that, like the law, what matters with grace in relationships is how it is received rather than whatever intentions lie behind it. Which is good news, since even when our actions are unconscious, and the Holy Spirit is guiding our hands, our motives are always mixed. What follows, then, is not an application section—*application* is almost always a code word for *law*. Implication would be more appropriate. Hopefully even inspiration.

GRACE IN FAMILIES

One-way love is often what distinguishes a warm household from a cold one. Children often move across the country to get away from a toxic home life where two-way conditionality has come to rule the roost via the judgments of parents and other siblings. A house full of conditions feels like a prison. Rules are one thing—take out the trash; don't hit your brother. They govern the day-to-day and protect us from one another. Conditions are different and more emotional in nature. "If you really loved us, then you wouldn't spend so much time with those people." "We will approve of whatever career choice you make, provided it's between medicine, law, and business." "Why can't you be more like your sister?" Even small differences between family members can be the source of tremendous friction. Yet grace has the power to bind generations together.

I am fortunate to have experienced the power of one-way love not just from my parents but my grandparents as well. In fact, whenever people learn that I was kicked out of the house at sixteen, they invariably ask how my grandparents responded. What they usually mean is "How did Billy and Ruth Graham respond to actual sin in their midst?" People looked up to them, not just as spiritual leaders, but as role models for how to raise godly children and grandchildren. "Weren't you shaming the family name?" The truth is, my grandparents never said a single word to me about getting my act together. They never pulled me aside at a family gathering and told me about how I needed to submit myself to Jesus, etc. Never. Only God knows what they were thinking or feeling, but I never picked up on a shred of judgment from them. They treated me exactly the opposite of how I deserved to be treated.

For example, I wore earrings back in those days. One in the left, and one in the right. It used to drive my parents nuts. Every time my grandmother—Ruth Graham—came down to visit, she would bring me a fresh set of earrings to wear! They were always funny. At Christmastime, she would bring me ornament earrings and make me put them in and take a picture. At Thanksgiving, she brought fork and knife earrings, and she took a picture. She made light of it. She wasn't making fun of me. She was saying, "This isn't that big of a deal. He's going to grow out of it." It may sound pretty trivial, but it meant the world to me. Everyone else was on my case, and instead of giving me one more thing to rebel against, my grandparents drew me in closer.

GRACE IN MARRIAGE

A marriage is a like a petri dish for the weight of conditionality and the beauty of one-way love. Husbands and wives are often so hard on one another, merciless with their demands and expectations, their criticisms and silences. And yet what brought the couple together in the first place was almost always an experience of grace, some connection that transcended their worthiness. As Southern novelist Walker Percy writes in *Love in the Ruins*, "We love those who know the worst of us and don't turn their faces away."[6]

A marriage founded on one-way love eschews scorekeeping at all costs. It is not a fifty-fifty proposition, where I scratch your back and then you scratch mine. A grace-centered marriage is one in which both partners give 100 percent of themselves. They give up their right to talk about rights. This means that a grace-centered marriage, in theory, is one where both parties are constantly apologizing to each other, asking for and granting forgiveness. No one is ever innocent in a grace-centered marriage. If original sin is as evenly distributed as the Bible claims it is, then even in the most extreme and wounding circumstances, both parties have some culpability.

So often an apology feels like we are betraying ourselves, does it not? We would rather see a marriage fall apart than admit to any wrongdoing or cede any ground in the "war of the roses." The world tells us to stand up for ourselves, to stick to our guns. But the Gospel tells us to lay down our arms. There is nothing at stake, and therefore nothing to fear, ultimately. Our righteousness, which we are often hell-bent on protecting in a marriage, has already been secured, and it is not our own. This doesn't mean we let the other person run all over us—we are not Jesus after all!—it simply means that for the marriage founded on one-way love, there is always a way forward.

In 2009, Laura Munson wrote a remarkable reflection on the near dissolution of her marriage for *The New York Times* titled "Those Aren't Fighting Words, Dear" that captures part of what we

are talking about better than any explicitly Christian testimony I've
ever come across. She recounts a painful afternoon when her husband of thirty years came to her, out of the blue, to tell her that he
didn't love her anymore and wanted out of the marriage. She writes,
"[My husband's] words came at me like a speeding fist, like a sucker
punch, yet somehow in that moment I was able to duck. And once
I recovered and composed myself, I managed to say, 'I don't buy it.'
Because I didn't."

Instead of rising to his hurtful words and responding in kind,
she surprised even herself by holding her tongue. She knew that
her husband was going through a tough time in his career, feeling
less than good about himself, and more than likely transferring that
inadequacy onto their relationship. But it's one thing to understand
these things intellectually and another to in the moment:

> You can bet I wanted to sit him down and persuade
> him to stay. To love me. To fight for what we've
> created. You can bet I wanted to.
>
> But I didn't.
>
> I barbecued. Made lemonade. Set the table for
> four. Loved him from afar.
>
> And one day, there he was, home from work
> early, mowing the lawn. A man doesn't mow his
> lawn if he's going to leave it. Not this man. Then
> he fixed a door that had been broken for eight years
> … He mentioned needing wood for next winter.
> The future. Little by little, he started talking about
> the future.

He wasn't happy about any of this, and it wasn't a walk in the park for Kim, me, or the other kids either. It actually made things harder. Without his phone and his friends, he haunted the house like a drug addict going through detox. He couldn't help out by giving his brother and sister rides, so Kim and I had to go back to serving as chauffeurs.

A month or so after the clampdown had gone into effect, I was traveling back from a conference. Before I left, I had told my son, in my most earnest, authoritative-father voice, that there was only one thing he needed to do while I was gone and that was to not give his mother a hard time. If he didn't give her any unnecessary headaches, when I got back, we might revisit the phone issue. Midway through my trip, I received a call from Kim, who told me that my request was not, shall we say, being respected.

I spent the plane ride home battling with God. I mean, really going back and forth with Him about what I should do. I knew I had to deal with the situation as soon as I returned. I was angry with my son for putting me in this situation, and I was tired of dealing with his ingratitude. But more than that, I wasn't ready to give up control. Not remotely. And if there's anything the law affords, it's control.

Yet as I prayed about it, I felt that the Lord was clearly telling me that, despite appearances, it was time to relent. Time to give the boy his phone back. Every fiber of my being was resistant to such an action. I was afraid of what my son would do with his freedom. I know what I had always done in those situations—taken advantage—and I was too smart and too prideful to allow that to happen to me. Plus, he didn't deserve to get his phone back. The one thing I had asked him to do, he hadn't done. He'd understood the condition before I left: be good, and you'll get a phone. Well, he hadn't been good. So no phone. Very reasonable to me. I was looking for an excuse, any excuse, to keep the handcuffs on. That I was flying back from a conference where I had spoken about one-way love was not lost on me.

Well, I got home, called my son out of his room, and told him we needed to talk. I reminded him of everything I'd said before I left—the conditions under which he would get a phone. He looked at me very sheepishly, knowing he was guilty—again! I talked to him for a few minutes about life and choices and how much we loved him. He listened intently. Then I looked at him and said, "Now put your shoes on, and let's go to the phone store and get you a new phone."

He was completely shocked. His lip started to quiver, and he finally burst into tears. I asked him what was wrong. With tears streaming down his face, he looked at me and said, "But, Dad, I don't deserve a phone."

He was right. He didn't deserve a phone. He didn't deserve a pad of paper and a stamp. His words revealed that God knew a lot better than I how to handle my son. The contrition was genuine. The law had leveled him. It had shown him who he was in a way that left no doubt about his need. It was time for the Gospel, so to speak.

Notice that his humility did not precede the invitation. The chronology is crucial. His admission was not a condition for mercy; it was its fruit!

I looked at him and said, "Listen, son. God takes me to the phone store ten thousand times a day, and I have never ever deserved one."

It was a happy day.

Now, before you line up to give me the father-of-the-year award, know that the reason I tell the story is because it was such a surprise to me too. My son had come by his rebelliousness honestly, after all. One of the main reasons his behavior bugged me so much was that he reminded me so much of myself—only he was so much sweeter! No, I am the chief of sinners here. I only tell the story for three reasons: One, it illustrates that the law *is* useful. But two, it illustrates how resistant we are to grace. We feel much safer with our hands on the wheel. I was so afraid that he would go nuts, that he would prove himself to be his father's son once again. It was as hard for me to give up the sense of manageability the law provided as it was for him to lose his phone. It had to be taken from me. Three, the emotional response at being let off the hook was a powerful reminder that only grace can accomplish what the law demands, namely, only grace can produce a contrite heart.

To be clear, this does not mean that children never benefit from consequences. Of course not! My son certainly did. He needed the law to crush him. But then he needed a word of grace to cure him. Properly distinguishing the role and function of law and grace in parenting is crucial. I've tried to make clear throughout this book that both God's Law and God's Gospel are good and necessary, but both do very different things. Serious confusion—in both theology and daily life—happens when we fail to understand their distinct job descriptions. We'll wrongly depend on the law to do what only the Gospel can do, and vice versa.

So, for example, in order to function as a community of five in our home, rules need to be established—laws need to be put in place.

Our three kids know they can't steal from one another. They have to share the computer. Since harmonious relationships depend on trust, they can't lie. Because we have three cars and four drivers, my boys can't simply announce that they are taking one of the cars. They have to ask ahead of time. And so on and so forth. Rules are necessary.

Still, Kim and I are under no illusions that telling them what they can and cannot do over and over again can change their hearts and make them *want* to comply. When one of our kids throws a temper tantrum (typically Genna), thereby breaking one of the rules, we can send her to her room and take away some of her privileges. And we do. But while this may rightly produce sorrow at the revelation of her sin, it does not have the power to remove her sin. In other words, the law can crush her, but it cannot cure her—it can kill its object, but it cannot make it alive. If Kim and I don't follow up law with grace, Genna would be left without hope—defeated but not delivered. The Law illuminates sin but is powerless to eliminate sin. That's not part of its job description. It points to righteousness but can't produce it. It shows us what godliness is, but it cannot make us godly.

One final example, and we'll move on.

At a dinner one evening, my friend Dr. Rod Rosenbladt told me a true story of how he'd wrecked his car when he was sixteen years old. Rod had been drinking, and in fact, he and his friends were all drunk. After the accident, Rod called his dad and the first thing his dad asked him was, "Are you all right?" Rod assured him that he was fine. Then he confessed to his father that he was drunk. Rod was naturally terrified about how his father might respond. Later that night, after Rod had made it home, he wept and wept in his father's study. He was embarrassed, ashamed, and guilty. At the end of the ordeal, his father asked him this question: "How about tomorrow we go and get you a new car?"

Rod now says—and he has lived a lot of life, being nearly seventy at the time of this writing—that he became a Christian in that moment. God's Grace became real to him in that moment of forgiveness and mercy. Rod has since spent his life as a servant of Christ, as spokesman for the theology of grace at Concordia Seminary and cohost on the *White Horse Inn* radio program. Rod's father's grace didn't turn Rod into a drunk—it made him love his father and the Lord he served.

Now let me ask you: what would you like to say to Rod's dad? Rod says that every time he tells that story in public, there are always people in the audience who get angry. They say, "Your dad let you get away with that? He didn't punish you at all? What a great opportunity for your dad to teach you responsibility!"

Rod always chuckles when he hears that response and says, "Do you think I didn't know what I had done? Do you think it wasn't the most painful moment of my whole life up to that point? I was ashamed; I was scared. My father spoke grace to me in a moment when I knew I deserved wrath … and I came alive."

Isn't that the nature of grace? We know that we deserve punishment and then, when we receive mercy instead, we discover grace. Romans 5:8 reads, "While we were yet sinners, Christ died for us" (KJV). God gives us Grace. He gives forgiveness and imputes righteousness to us while we are weak, ungodly, sinful; while we are His enemies (Rom. 5:6, 8, 10). Our offenses are infinitely greater than a sixteen-year-old getting drunk and wrecking his car, yet God boasts about pouring out His one-way love on His undeserving children.

No one had to tell Rod to be sorry for his foolishness. No one had to tell Rod to be thankful that his dad didn't repay him "as his sins deserved." That one act of grace and mercy transformed him—and his whole life was changed by it. Because that's what grace does. It is the only thing that can transform entitled boys and girls into grateful men and women.

So hurry up and throw on some shoes. The car's running and the phone store awaits.

CHAPTER 8

AN OFFENSIVE GIFT

The legendary antagonist of Hugo's *Les Misérables* is the unrelenting and supremely competent inspector Javert. When we initially meet him, Javert is serving as a guard at the jail where Jean Valjean is imprisoned. When Valjean is given parole, it is Javert who insists that no matter where he goes or what he does, he will always be defined as a criminal. After the plot details recounted in chapter 4, Valjean breaks his parole and eventually assumes a false identity as mayor of a small town. A few years later, Javert, now promoted to the rank of inspector, recognizes his former prisoner and makes it his personal vendetta to bring him to justice. He does his job, but Valjean eludes him.

To say that Inspector Javert is committed to the rigorous inflexibility of the law would be an understatement. Javert does more than enforce the law—he embodies it. Indeed, mankind's relationship with the law was actually one of the main themes of the book,

according to Victor Hugo himself.[1] When they adapted the work for
the stage, Alain Boublil and Claude-Michel Schönberg made this
very clear. "Mine is the way of the law," Javert sings early on.

Valjean refuses to play by the same rules of quid pro quo, going
so far as to be gracious with Javert in their several encounters.
Valjean's treatment of him haunts and radically disorients Javert. In
the climatic scene, instead of doing away with him once and for all,
Valjean saves Javert's life. Javert is utterly undone by this unexpected
act of mercy. Hugo's description of his inner conflict captures the
offense of grace at its most visceral:

> Jean Valjean confused him. All the axioms that had
> served as the supports of his life crumbled away
> before this man. Jean Valjean's generosity toward
> him, Javert, overwhelmed him…. Javert felt that
> something horrible was penetrating his soul, admi-
> ration for a convict…. A beneficent malefactor, a
> compassionate convict, kind, helpful, clement,
> returning good for evil, returning pardon for hatred,
> loving pity rather than vengeance, preferring to
> destroy himself rather than destroy his enemy, sav-
> ing the one who had struck him, kneeling on the
> heights of virtue, nearer angels than men. Javert
> was compelled to acknowledge that this monster
> existed.
>
> This could not go on….
>
> All that [Javert] believed in was dissipat-
> ing. Truths he had no wish for besieged him

inexorably.... Authority was dead in him. He had
no further reason for being.[2]

The Law is ironclad. It does not make exceptions. It cannot
abide mercy. Like a robot being given a directive that contradicts
its programming, the law-addicted person has a complete meltdown
when shown grace. Which is precisely what happened to Javert. In
the same scene in the musical, he sings:

Damned if I'll live in the debt of a thief ...
I am the Law and the Law is not mocked ...
Granting me my life today
this man has killed me even so.[3]

For Javert, as with all of us, the logic of law makes sense. He
has lived his entire life according to the if-then conditionality:
if you do wrong, then you must be punished. This makes him,
and us, feel safe. It's easy to comprehend. It promotes a sense of
manageability. And best of all, it keeps him, and us, in control.
We get to keep our ledgers and scorecards. Javert would rather
die than deal with the disorienting reality of the one-way love he
receives from Valjean—so he jumps into the river, ending his life.
He chooses death over grace, control over chaos.

Like Javert, we are, by nature, allergic to grace. The logic of
grace is deeply offensive to our law-locked hearts. In fact, it isn't
really logic at all. It is more of a counterintuition that turns everything upside down and inside out. If the law says, "Good people
get good stuff; bad people get bad stuff," then grace says, "The

bad get the best; the worst inherit the wealth; the slave becomes a son."

Our initial response to one-way love tends to be one of shock and suspicion. We hear, "Of course you don't deserve it, but I'm giving it to you anyway." We wonder, *What is this really about? What's the catch?* Internal bells and alarms start to go off, and we begin saying, "Wait a minute.... This sounds too good to be true." Like Javert, we wonder about the ulterior motives of the excessively generous. What's in it for Him? After all, who could trust in or believe something so radically unbelievable?

But perhaps, like Javert, our defenses and suspicions are finally overwhelmed, and we are brought face-to-face with the extent of this free gift. When we do, we may find that disbelief is replaced by fear. Grace violates our deepest sense of justice and rightness, and like Javert, we are scared to death when grace wrests control completely out of our hands. In fact, life according to the law no longer makes sense in light of grace. Fearful of what kind of chaos would ensue if we abandoned ourselves wholly to its radicality, we cling to control—we stick with what we know so well, with what comes naturally. And just like Javert, we choose death over freedom.

Of course, the offensiveness of grace is not limited to literature. It is one of the main themes of the Bible. As we all know, Jesus encountered massive amounts of resistance to his ministry; indeed, his message is what got him killed. Grace was enormously threatening to the status quo then, just as it is today. As much as we might crave it when we are at the end of our rope, one-way love runs counter to the natural inclinations of the human heart. As this chapter seeks to illuminate, we see its offensiveness born out in the Bible, in the church, and in our everyday lives.

A RUINED DINNER PARTY

> One of the Pharisees asked [Jesus] to eat with him, and he went into the Pharisee's house and reclined at the table. And behold, a woman of the city, who was a sinner, when she learned that he was reclining at table in the Pharisee's house, brought an alabaster flask of ointment, and standing behind him at his feet, weeping, she began to wet his feet with her tears and wiped them with the hair of her head and kissed his feet and anointed them with the ointment. Now when the Pharisee who had invited him saw this, he said to himself, "If this man were a prophet, he would have known who and what sort of woman this is who is touching him, for she is a sinner." (Luke 7:36–39)

To grasp the depth of the offense we read of here, we need to understand a few things about social mores in the ancient Near East. From their earliest years, girls were instructed in proper etiquette. They were warned by their mothers about what happened to women who ignored the rules. Those women were the kind of women other women would shun. They weren't welcome in "nice" society, and self-respecting men disdained them. They had to hide during the day and do whatever work they did under the cover of night. And if they ever once decided that they might want to get right with God, there wasn't really any avenue open to them. Once a woman was marked as being immoral, beyond the pale, a sinner, she was and always would be an outcast.

Today, there are social programs to help women like this. And yet in some ways, we've romanticized the background of women who are down-and-out. We tend to look at them with pity and wonder what drove them to this sad end. You would never have found that kind of pathos surrounding immoral women in Israel. Think more along the lines of the disdain that celebrities like Lindsay Lohan inspire these days. Today we throw rocks via online character assassination and paparazzi sensationalism. Back then, they threw actual rocks. Ouch!

YOUR REPUTATION PRECEDES YOU

Notice the names and lack thereof. We are given the name of the Pharisee who had invited Jesus for dinner, Simon, but the name of the woman who barges in goes unrecorded. Perhaps because it does not need to be. She is known by reputation, "the" immoral woman, "the" sinner. When news of this encounter gets out, it is very likely that nobody wonders, even for a moment, who the "she" is.

Now, not only was this woman despised for her lifestyle, she was evidently unafraid of adding fuel to the fire. First, she entered Simon's home uninvited and unaccompanied. "Who does she think she is? How dare she?" everyone in attendance would have murmured in shocked dismay. This was the *last* person you would want coming to a dinner party. She wasn't crashing just any dinner party—it was a party at the home of a religious leader, a Pharisee, a holy man, the opposite of a place where she might conceivably be welcome. So here she came, this epitome of everything a woman should not be—rebellious, promiscuous, uncouth, foolish, and very likely diseased—and she threw herself down at the feet of Simon's guest. Why didn't she just wait for Jesus outside or try to catch him beforehand? Why wasn't she afraid of what would happen?

Her brazenness didn't end there. No, the indignities just kept multiplying. Out from under her soiled robes, she brought an alabaster flask of ointment. Onlookers could easily surmise where she had gotten the money to buy it and for what purposes she had previously used it. But now she fell behind a reclining Jesus, while Simon, the disciples, and even the house slaves stood aghast. She poured her precious perfume on Jesus's feet. Then she uncovered her head (another religious no-no), took down her hair, and used her hair as a towel to clean him. Apparently she wept so intensely that her tears made a bath for his calloused, dry feet. And then she kissed him. Over and over again. *And he welcomed it. Jesus welcomed the kisses of a whore.* She, the defiled, was cleaning Jesus, the pure.

Again, you have to ask yourself, "What was she thinking, pulling such a bold move? How did she think those men would respond? How did she think Jesus would respond? What was her hope? And where did she get the courage to do such a thing?" Clearly, this woman had come to the end of herself. Like an addict hitting bottom, she had died to everything but her desire for help. She ran to Christ, and he did not turn her away. Grace begins where pride ends.

The scene offended those who witnessed it. And it did not offend them because they were overly prudish or hyperreligious—although they probably were. Grace offends because it *is* offensive. Unlike every other kind of love there is, one-way love does not depend on our loveliness. It precedes loveliness. And while we see it mirrored in countless ways in our daily lives and relationships, the Gospel is the only place where we find this kind of paradigm-shattering grace in its pure, unadulterated state. Jesus is its starting point, and yet we must never forget that it got him crucified.

FINALLY AND FULLY FORGIVEN

"Your sins are forgiven. Your faith has saved you; go in peace." *Wait—whaaat?* In response to Jesus's words, Simon and the other guests sitting around the table were knocked off their theological high horses. *Who is this man that he can forgive sins?* they all wondered. Of course, at that point, Jesus was not terribly concerned about answering their questions. Right then, he was binding to himself a woman who had been lost and was now found.

Note that we don't have any record of her saying anything like, "I'm really sorry. I promise to live a reformed life from now on." We don't have a record of her saying anything at all! All we have a record of her doing is kissing his feet, washing them with her tears, and drying them with her hair. No promises to do better. No declarations of her own fidelity and determination to live a changed life. No Sinner's Prayer prayed; no resolutions signed. Just tears and kisses and audacious love.

I remember a recently divorced woman who came to me for counseling. She was consumed by anger at her ex-husband, and it was spilling out into her relationships with everyone around her, including her children. She had plenty of reason to be mad. He had treated her terribly and then abandoned her at a particularly vulnerable time. You could not blame her for her anger.

After she finished sharing, I asked if she thought there was any possibility of forgiveness.

"Forgive him? He would never ask for forgiveness! And unless he asked for it, I would never grant it. And even then, I'd have to really believe it, you know? I'd have to see some real change. We are only called to forgive those who have repented. That's how God works."

Oh, really? I remember thinking at the time.

Now, there are plenty of reasons why she might not forgive or be able to forgive her ex-husband, but invoking God as her example would not be one of them. If God forgave only those who sincerely repented and changed their ways, it would be a very short list. "While we were yet sinners" is how the apostle Paul put it (Rom. 5:8 KJV). In her victimhood and woundedness, this woman had lost sight of the fact that God had forgiven her—and continued to forgive her—in the midst of her sin and pride, lost sight of the fact that if He waited for her to straighten out, He would wait forever.

At this point, you may be wondering whether Jesus granted forgiveness to the woman at the dinner because of something he saw in her. You may be wondering if it was her display of love that procured her salvation, rather than his outrageous grace. In anticipation of our question, Luke 7:47 teaches us that her forgiveness wasn't the result

of her love, but rather the cause of it. Jesus told her that her faith in
the forgiveness he had already granted was what ultimately saved her.
It is what saves us, too, thank God.

ANOTHER LOST SOUL

Although it was shocking to the people in attendance, I am guessing
that Jesus's response to this woman doesn't offend us much. Perhaps
we feel sorry for the woman. We know she was a victim of forces
outside her control—no one *chooses* to become a prostitute, after all.
Or perhaps we are just used to Jesus's compassion for sinners. Truth
be told, in our day and age, it is not really the story of the immoral
woman that is so shocking. It is Christ's interaction with Simon the
Pharisee that gives us pause. Indeed, there was more than one person
at that dinner party in need of saving.

We don't know why Simon invited Jesus to dine with him.
Perhaps as a high-ranking member of the religious elite, he
thought it was his social obligation. Perhaps he had a secret hope
that Jesus was the Messiah and that he would be the first to herald
him. Maybe he was suspicious and looking for a way to discredit
Jesus in the eyes of his fellow villagers. Or perhaps he wanted Jesus
to see how righteous *he* was and to honor *him*. We don't know. We
only know that Simon was not overly welcoming to Jesus when he
arrived, refusing to offer him the customary gestures of cleansing
water, a kiss, or anointing oil. But like every other encounter Jesus
had with the uninitiated, we know that Simon's life was about to
be completely inverted. What might have begun as a search for a
flattering word, a burning curiosity, or an embellished reputation

ended up demolishing everything Simon thought he knew about God.

Simon's assumption, of course, was that if Jesus knew this woman was immoral, he wouldn't let her near him. But there was another, more insidious assumption hidden in his presuppositions: *She's different from me. She is a sinner, and I am not.* It probably never crossed his mind that Jesus had to condescend to come into *Simon's* house just as much as he did to receive this woman's kisses. Simon's problem was that he thought he didn't have a problem. Not surprisingly, this is what we call *pharisaism*.

The miracle is that Jesus had great love for this self-righteous zealot and was determined to rescue him:

> And Jesus answering said to him, "Simon, I have something to say to you." And he answered, "Say it, Teacher."
>
> "A certain moneylender had two debtors. One owed five hundred denarii, and the other fifty. When they could not pay, he cancelled the debt of both. Now which of them will love him more?" Simon answered, "The one, I suppose, for whom he cancelled the larger debt." And he said to him, "You have judged rightly." Then turning toward the woman he said to Simon, "Do you see this woman? I entered your house; you gave me no water for my feet, but she has wet my feet with her tears and wiped them with her hair. You gave me no kiss, but from the time I came in she has

not ceased to kiss my feet. You did not anoint my head with oil, but she has anointed my feet with ointment. Therefore I tell you, her sins, which are many, are forgiven—for she loved much. But he who is forgiven little, loves little." And he said to her, "Your sins are forgiven." Then those who were at table with him began to say among themselves, "Who is this, who even forgives sins?" And he said to the woman, "Your faith has saved you; go in peace." (Luke 7:40–50)

Three sentences. One question. Complete annihilation. Neither debtor was able to repay their debt. So the debt, if it was to be addressed at all, had to be cancelled via the generosity of the moneylender. It is as if the Lord said, "Simon, you're the primary debtor here. I have cancelled your great debt, but your love for me is paltry, because you don't think you owe me much. And when it comes to real righteousness, true obedience, you, a student of the Law, know that love from the heart is all that ultimately matters. What you do not understand is that right now, this immoral woman is more righteous than you are, because she loves and you don't. *You need to learn from her.*"

Learn from *her*? On this side of the story, it's nearly impossible for us to understand the shock and offense that Simon must have felt. Simon's discomfort at this point was obvious by his equivocating answer: "Well ... I suppose ... the one who had been forgiven for much loved much...." This man, who just one moment ago thought he had all the answers, was now hedging.

But once Jesus had begun, he wouldn't stop until Simon was completely undone. In lawyerlike fashion, Jesus proceeded, point by point, through all of Simon's breaches of hospitality. Simon hadn't been gracious with Jesus, because he had a falsely high view of himself. Perhaps he thought Jesus should have been grateful! Simon did not know himself. He thought he had no need of grace. He was enamored with his own "righteousness."

Then, in case Simon thought he should have just been a bit more courteous to his guest, Jesus forgave the immoral woman's sin. This act left Simon completely speechless. The Bible doesn't tell us anything more about Simon, but one thing we can safely assume is that he was never the same. The rescue project had begun. Perhaps he found rest for his troubled conscience in the grace of the Savior who welcomed the kisses of both harlots and Pharisees, or perhaps he spent his days in despair and self-recrimination. I pray it was the former.

STOCKHOLM SYNDROME

There is nothing harder for us to wrap our minds around than the unconditional, noncontingent grace of God. As it did with Simon and Javert, one-way love upends our sense of fairness and offends our deepest instincts. We insist that reality operate according to the predictable economy of reward and punishment, especially when it comes to those who have done us harm.

Even those of us who have tasted the radical saving grace of God find it intuitively difficult *not* to put conditions on it when we try to communicate it to others—"Don't take it too far; keep it balanced." As understandable as this hedging tendency may be, a "yes grace, but" posture perpetuates slavery in our lives and in the church. Grace is radically unbalanced. It contains no but: it is unconditional, uncontrollable, unpredictable, and undomesticated—or else it is not grace. As Doug Wilson put it recently, "Grace is wild. Grace unsettles everything. Grace overflows the banks. Grace messes up your hair. Grace is not tame. In fact, unless we are making the devout nervous, we are not preaching grace as we ought."[4]

The truth is, we all have a bit of the self-righteous older brother in the parable of the prodigal son inside us. Remember the elder brother? The one who worked for years and never outwardly disrespected his father but was incensed when his father welcomed his wayward younger brother back to the fold. The elder brother's reaction revealed that he had more in common with his sibling than he realized: neither of them loved the father. When the elder brother saw the father giving away part of the inheritance he thought he deserved, his true motivations became evident. "You welcome this prostitute-visiting, decadent louse home with a fattened calf, but you never once gave me even a goat to party with!"

Of course, we might ask why the son never asked for a goat or a calf or a party. He did not ask, because he thought of his father as an employer, and no good employee asks their boss to throw a party for them. In the end, of course, the prodigal son was welcomed home while his older, self-righteous brother stood alone in the courtyard, fuming with bitterness. His offense at the grace his brother received stranded him out in the cold, away from the joyful celebration inside, which is where the story leaves him.

So it often is with us. The storm may be raging all around us, our foundations may be shaking, but we would rather perish than give up our "rights." We have worked too hard for that! Gerhard Forde puts it like this:

> You see, we really are sealed up in the prison of our conditional thinking. It is terribly difficult for us to get out, and even if someone batters down the door and shatters the bars, chances are we will stay in the prison anyway! We seem always to want to hold out for something somehow, that little bit of something, and we do it with a passion and an anxiety that betrays its true source—the Old Adam that just does not want to lose control.[5]

I wish I couldn't relate. Recently Kim and I were reflecting on our current season in life, which often feels like a grind. We are raising three children, two teenaged boys and a girl who will be a teenager soon—meaning, we are in the thick of it. In just a few short months, our eldest son, Gabe, will be off to college. In the midst of the sometimes-overwhelming complexity of everything we are facing, I found myself wondering, *Why, in the midst of all this pressure, in this crucible of such challenge, am I still so opposed to grace? Why?*

The answer—surprise, surprise—has to do with control. I feel like I have got to maintain control of things. I've got to keep everything in order, because if I don't, things are going to spin into chaos. What a faithless and hypocritical way to operate!

As much as I sometimes wish it were not the case, this is not some abstract truth I am trying to convey. I experience the struggle between control and grace every day. Believe me, there are many days when I would prefer to have a to-do list. Like you, I long for the comfort that a checklist brings, something to assure me that everything will work out the way I want it to—if I can just do what is asked of me. I want protection from self-doubt. I yearn for power over others, myself, and yes, even God. Ultimately I want to be my own rescuer, to save myself. The law allows me to keep help, deliverance, salvation, and rescue right where I want them: on my own keyboard, within reach. So I resist the Gospel, because I don't want to give up control; indeed, because I can't. Like a hostage suffering from Stockholm syndrome, I am in love with the very thing that is keeping me enslaved. As The Replacements once sang, "Someone take the wheel"!

There is no way around it: God's one-way love is deeply offensive. Frightening even. So much so that if you're not offended by it, you probably haven't encountered the real thing.

Grace turns our world upside down. It disrespects our values, pops the bubble of our self-righteousness, suspends reciprocity, and introduces chaos. It throws our to-do lists out the window. But perhaps the scariest and most offensive part of all is the question it asks. It is a question we spend a good amount of time and energy running away from, one whose answer most of us have long since abdicated to our idols. Listen closely or you'll miss it: now that you don't have to prove anything to anyone, now that your self-regard and self-respect have been unassailably secured, now that your actions have been unhitched from their utility in the courtroom, and you have been fully justified in the sight of God … What do you *want* to do?

What are you going to do now that you don't *have* to do anything?

I'm serious. Think about it, if only for that brief moment before the voices of responsibility kick in and dismiss your freedom as a flight of fancy or something too dangerous to be embraced. My suspicion is that once you realize that you don't *have* to do anything for God, you may find you *want* to do everything for Him.

CHAPTER 9

OBJECTIONS TO ONE-WAY LOVE

For many Americans of a certain age, the college admissions process is an oppressive and extraordinarily stressful area of life. It is performancism writ very, very large. One's entire worth and value as a person is boiled down to a short transcript and application, which is then judged according to a stringent and ever-escalating set of standards. High school seniors are called upon to justify themselves according to their achievements and interests, and as the top schools have gotten more and more competitive, so has the pressure under which our top students place themselves. Watching the students at our church go through it, not to mention my own kids, it's hard not to sympathize. They feel that their entire lives are hanging in the balance, that where they go to school will dictate their happiness for years to come.

A couple of years ago, I watched as two best friends, Wayne and Dave, applied for early admission to the same college. That December, Wayne was accepted and Dave was deferred. The next four months, during which Dave waited for the final ruling, looked very different—and very similar—for each of them. They both took basically the same classes and had the same homework load. They spent time with many of the same people socially. But there were also a couple of key differences. No longer under the watchful eye of the all-important transcript, Wayne decided to branch out in his extracurricular activities. He started a band and got into rock climbing. He even pioneered a program teaching underprivileged kids in the community how to climb. The program still exists, more than ten years later. Meanwhile, Dave got involved in a bunch of extracurriculars he had never been involved with before, stuff that he thought might boost his chances at getting into his dream college.

By the end of the semester, Dave was exhausted, and Wayne was full of energy. Although Dave did well and kept up his GPA, Wayne got the best grades of his high school career! Freed from having to play it safe, he wrote his papers about topics he was genuinely interested in rather than the ones he thought the teacher would appreciate, and it showed on the page. Their paths may not have looked very different to the outside eye, but one of these guys was carrying a burden of expectation and one wasn't. No wonder it felt like such a slog.

The fruit of assurance in Wayne's life was not laziness but creativity, charity, and fun. Set free from the imperative to perform, his performance shot off the charts. Set free from having to earn his future, he enjoyed his present. Set free from the burden of self-focus, he was inspired to serve others—and without being told he needed to do so! This is very similar to the dynamic we saw at work with the apostle Peter and with Zacchaeus, the same one we see with many of those that Jesus heals.

The message of God's one-way love for sinners naturally meets resistance from law-addled hearts. It produces objections in those who are wired for earning and deserving, which is all of us. Sometimes these objections are rationalized forms of the emotional offense that we looked at in the last chapter. When our sense of pride is attacked, it defends. Sometimes these objections are projections of fear about what might happen if people actually believed the message. Sometimes the objections to grace are simply honest rejoinders to a word that can be very hard to swallow.

Two of the most frequent objections I encounter—and I encounter them a lot—are that grace makes people lazy and grace gives people license to sin and/or indulge in their self-absorption rather than serve their neighbors. While by no means exhaustive, this chapter seeks to shed some light on both of these strands of protestation.

DOES GRACE MAKE YOU LAZY?

First, the laziness accusation. If it is true that Jesus paid it all, that "it is finished," that my value, worth, security, freedom, justification, and so on is forever fixed, then why do anything? Doesn't grace undercut ambition? Doesn't the Gospel weaken effort? If we are truly let off the hook, what is to stop us from ending up like George Costanza in the "Summer of George" episode of the sitcom *Seinfeld* when he received an unexpected severance package and vowed to take full advantage of his freedom only to sit around in sweatpants, watching TV, reading comic books, and eating "a big hunk of cheese like it's an apple"? Or, as Billy Corgan, lead singer of Smashing Pumpkins, is reported to have once pondered, "If practice makes perfect, and no one's perfect, then why practice?" Understandable question.

To be perfectly honest, in the short term, this message often *does* inspire the kind of sighs of relief and extended breathers that look a whole lot like nothing. But if a person can be given the space to bask in the Good News for a while (without being hammered with fresh injunctions), we just as often find that the Gospel of grace, in the long run, actually empowers risk-taking effort and neighbor-embracing love. It doesn't *have* to, of course, which is precisely why it does. Think about it: what prevents us from taking great risks most of the time is the fear that if we don't succeed, we will lose out on something we need in order to be happy. And so we live life playing our cards close to the chest … relationally, vocationally, spiritually. We measure our investments carefully because we need a return—we are afraid to give, because it might not work out, and we *need* it to work out.

The refrain repeated throughout this book is that everything we need, we already possess in Christ. This means that the what-if has been taken out of the equation. We can take absurd risks, push harder, go further, and leave it all on the field without fear—and have fun doing so. We can give with reckless abandon, because we no longer need to ensure a return of success, love, meaning, validation, and approval. We can invest freely and forcefully, because we've been freely and forcefully invested in. Perhaps this is part of why rates of charitable giving are so much higher in places where people go to church. Perhaps not.

The Gospel breaks the chains of reciprocity and the circular exchange. Since there is nothing we ultimately need from one another, we are free to do *everything* for one another. Spend our lives giving instead of taking; going to the back instead of getting to the front; sacrificing ourselves for others instead of sacrificing others for ourselves. The Gospel alone liberates us to live a life of scandalous generosity, unrestrained sacrifice, uncommon valor, and unbounded courage.

This is the difference between approaching all of life *from* salvation and approaching all of life *for* salvation; it's the difference between approaching life *from* our acceptance, and not *for* our acceptance; *from* love not *for* love. The acceptance letter has arrived, and it cannot be rescinded, thank God.

I remember reading an article about Netflix, the wildly successful video rental and streaming company, a few years ago that pointed to what we are talking about here. Netflix, it turns out, has no official vacation policy. They let their employees take as much time off as they want, whenever they want, as long as the job is getting done. The article quoted Netflix's vice president for corporate communication, Steve Swasey, as saying, "Rules and policies and regulations and stipulations are innovation killers. People do their best work when they're unencumbered. If you're spending a lot of time accounting for the time you're spending, that's time you're not innovating."[1] Their policy, or lack thereof, has not resulted in the company's going out of business, which many of us would fear it would. In fact, just the opposite. Freed from micromanaging bosses, their employees work even harder. Now, obviously, this is not the same thing as the assurance we have in Christ, but perhaps it is not so different either.

DECONSTRUCTING MORALISM (AND ANTINOMIANISM)

All right, so perhaps one-way love doesn't promote laziness, but if you are telling people they can do whatever they want, won't they … do whatever they want? Won't they indulge in all sorts of debauched behavior? There seems to be a fear out there that preaching grace produces serial killers. Or, to put it in more theological terms, too much emphasis on the indicatives of the Gospel leads to lawlessness.

Again, the formal name for the objection of lawlessness is *antinomianism*—preaching in such a way as to imply that the Law is bad and/or useless. If the control and laziness objections tend to come equally from the religious and nonreligious world, then the antinomianism objection comes almost exclusively from the religious sphere. After all, since our culture is already so permissive and morally lax, if we Christians don't stand up for God's standards of moral righteousness, His Law, then who will? Is more grace really what this culture needs? That doesn't make sense. It seems backward and counterintuitive. Unconditional pardon is probably the last thing lawless people need to hear, right? Surely they'll take advantage of it and get worse, not better. After all, it seems logical that the only way to "save" licentious people is to show them more rules, intensify the exhortations to behave.

Well, let's lay aside the obvious rejoinder that if the only reason you're not engaging in sex, drugs, and rock 'n' roll is out of fear, if your only motivation for obedience is threat, then perhaps you need to look at your own heart before you think about other people's. Let's also lay aside the fact that the Bible makes it explicitly clear that the power that saves even the worst rule-breaking sinner is the Gospel (Rom. 1:16) and not the Law (Rom. 7:13–24). There is another crucial reason why preaching the Gospel of free grace is both necessary and effective at a time when moralism is what reigns supreme: moralism is what far too many people already think Christianity is all about—rules and standards and behavior and cleaning yourself up.

Millions of people, both inside and outside the church, perceive the essential message of Christianity to be "If you behave, then you belong." The reason they come to that conclusion is because many of us preachers have led them to believe that. We have led them to believe that God is more interested in people becoming good than in them coming to terms with how needy and self-centered they actually are so that they'll fix their eyes on Christ, "the author and finisher of our faith" (Heb. 12:2 KJV).

From a human standpoint, this is precisely why many outside the church reject Christianity *and* why so many inside the church conk out: they're just not good enough to "get 'er done" over the long haul. Of course, there are also those who ignore the Gospel because they have deceived themselves into believing that they really are making it, when in reality they're not. But everyone peters out eventually, on their deathbed if not before. In his article "Preaching in a Post-modern Climate," Tim Keller makes this point brilliantly:

> Some claim that to constantly be striking a "note
> of grace, grace, grace" in our sermons is not helpful

in our culture today. The objection goes like this: "Surely Pharisaism and moralism is not a problem in our culture today. Rather, our problem is license and antinomianism. People lack a sense of right or wrong. It is 'carrying coal to Newcastle' to talk about grace all the time to postmodern people." But I don't believe that's the case. Unless you point to the "good news" of grace, people won't even be able to bear the "bad news" of God's judgment. Also, unless you critique moralism, many irreligious people won't know the difference between moralism and what you're offering. The way to get antinomians to move away from lawlessness is to distinguish the gospel from legalism. Why? Because modern and post-modern people have been rejecting Christianity for years thinking that it was indistinguishable from moralism. Non-Christians will always automatically hear gospel presentations as appeals to become moral and religious, *unless* in your preaching you use the good news of grace to deconstruct legalism. Only if you show them there's a difference—that what they *really* rejected wasn't real Christianity at all—will they even begin to consider Christianity.[2]

In Romans 6:1–4 the apostle Paul answers the charge of antinomianism (lawlessness) not with Law but with more Gospel! I imagine it would have been tempting for Paul (as it often is with us when dealing with licentious people) to put the brakes on grace and invoke the Law in this passage, but instead he gives more grace—grace upon grace. Paul knows that licentious people are not those who believe the Gospel of God's free grace too much, but too little. "The ultimate antidote to antinomianism," writes Michael Horton, "is *not* more imperatives, but the realization that the Gospel swallows the tyranny as well as the guilt of sin."[3]

The fact is, the only way any of us ever start to live a life of true obedience is when we get a taste of God's radical, unconditional acceptance of sinners. The message that justifies is the same message that sanctifies. What makes us think the same generosity that flows from the Gospel of forgiveness won't lead others to repentance the way it has us?

In chapter 4, we noted that Law without Gospel leads to licentiousness, not the opposite. I know this not only because I read it in the Bible, but because I've experienced it in my own life (see chapter 2) and see it in others all the time. The tragic and ironic thing about legalism is that it not only doesn't make people work harder, it makes them give up. Make no mistake, in the illustration that opened this chapter, if his deferral had continued indefinitely, poor Dave would have eventually hit the wall and walked away from the college process altogether. Over time, continued exhortations to live up to God's standard of moral perfection will inspire a "why even try?" response. Moralism will produce immorality, not the other way around. Just think about your own children. Or your relationship with your spouse.

This is not to say the Law is somehow bad—it is doing one of the things it is supposed to do, revealing need and sin! Don't think for a second that the Spirit doesn't use both of God's two words in our lives: the Law as well as the Gospel. It's just that, as we explored in earlier chapters, they do very different things. The Law *reveals* sin but cannot *remove* it. It *prescribes* righteousness but is powerless to *produce* it. The Law is impotent—it has no creative power, it cannot inspire. It offers us nothing but condemnation and death. The Law apart from the Gospel can only crush; it can't cure.

> The law says, Do, and life you'll win;
>   but grace says, Live, for all is done;
>   the former cannot ease my grief,
>   the latter yields me full relief.[4]

So the Law serves us by showing us how to love God and others. But we fail to do this every day. And when we fail, it is the Gospel that brings comfort by reminding us that God's infinite approval of us doesn't depend on our keeping of the Law but on Christ's keeping of the Law for us. And guess what? This makes me want to obey him more, not less! As Charles Spurgeon once wrote, "When I thought that God was hard, I found it easy to sin. But when I found God so kind, so good, so overflowing with compassion, I smote upon my breast to think that I could have rebelled against One who loved me so and sought my good."[5]

Ultimately, though, even if we wanted to be free of the Law, we never could be. It is written on the heart; it is a part of our DNA. Rebellion and conformity are simply two sides of the same coin. As Martin Luther wrote in his "Treatise Against Antinomians," "For if you resolve to [annul] the Law ... you do no more in effect, but throw away the poor letters *L.A.W...*."[6] Or as Gerhard Forde is reported to have observed, "We may leave the church, but the Law goes with us." Christian or non-Christian, the Law is as inescapable as oxygen. This is why Jady Koch writes, with tongue firmly in cheek, that "bigfoot called my unicorn an antinomian."[7] Bob Godfrey, president of Westminster Seminary in California, used to say in class that there have been many antinomian controversies throughout history, but in many cases the legalists won them by default, since the antinomians never showed. In other words, they're hypothetical in the truest sense.

These claims certainly line up with my nearly twenty years of ministry experience. I've never actually met anyone who has been truly gripped by God's amazing grace in the Gospel who is then so ungrateful that they don't care about respecting or obeying Him. But this is not to imply that my fellow believers' concerns are entirely unfounded.

MAKE A RULE OR BREAK A RULE

If the human propensity to self-justify is as widespread and deep-seated as the Bible claims it is, then we will use anything at our disposal in its service—even God's grace itself. Like entitled children, we will pervert and subvert the gift of God's one-way love to validate our self-centeredness, we will make grace into a new law. Our understanding of grace becomes a new righteousness of our own for us to wield like a weapon; we will use it like a shield to protect ourselves from the guilt and culpability the Law brings rather than as the only refuge from it. Remember, Christ came not to abolish the Law but to fulfill it.

What I think is going on in these situations, more often than not, is that these antinomians are not actually engaging in lawlessness but are wrapped up in a different form of legalism.

Spend any time in the American church, and you'll hear legalism and lawlessness presented as two ditches on either side of the Gospel that we must avoid. *Legalism*, they say, happens when you focus too much on Law (big L) or rules (little l), and *lawlessness* when you focus too much on grace. Therefore, in order to maintain spiritual equilibrium, you have to balance law and grace. If you start getting too much law, you need to balance it with grace. If you start getting too much grace, you need to balance it with law. I have come to believe that this "balanced" way of framing the issue can unwittingly keep us from really understanding the Gospel of grace in all of its radical depth and beauty.

It is more theologically accurate to say that the one primary enemy of the Gospel—legalism—comes in two forms. Some people avoid the Gospel and try to save themselves by keeping the rules, doing what they're told, maintaining the standards, and so on (you could call this "front-door legalism"). Other people avoid the Gospel and try to save themselves by breaking the rules, doing whatever they want, developing their own autonomous standards, and so on (you could call this "back-door legalism"). In other words, there are two "laws" that we typically choose from: the law that says, "I can find freedom and fullness of life if I keep the rules," or the law that says, "I can find freedom and fullness of life if I break the rules." Either way, you're still trying to save yourself—which means both are legalistic, because both are self-salvation projects. "Make a rule" or "break a rule" really belong to the same passion for autonomy (self-rule). We want to remain in control of our lives and our destinies, so the only choice is whether we will conquer the mountain by asceticism or by license. Again, in the strictest sense, true antinomianism is really the only impossible heresy: if people reject God's Law, they will simply replace it with one of their own making.

So it would be a mistake to identify the "two cliffs" as being legalism and lawlessness. What some call license is just another form of legalism. And if people outside the church are guilty of break-the-rules legalism, many people inside the church are still guilty of keep-the-rules legalism.

I make this diagnosis with such conviction, because I have engaged in both. You'll recall that I spent the first twenty-one years of my life trying to find my identity and righteousness by being "bad." At twenty-one, the God who loves sinners miraculously saved me, and I experienced a period of intense joy and gratitude. But then something unexpected began to happen. God's grace gradually, imperceptibly faded from importance, and my response to grace took its place as the focus of my life. Once again, what I was doing became preeminent. I began to try to find my righteousness, my identity, freedom, and fullness in life by *keeping* the rules.

Up until that point, I struggled with what is the typical non-Christian response to the rules: break as many as you can and with as much gusto as you can! Now, my struggle was with keeping the rules and, of course, making sure that everyone else did too. I actually came to believe (although I never would have said it in this way) that God would love me more if I was good and always colored inside the lines. I had my spiritual to-do list and relished every occasion to check something off it. Once again, I was building my own identity, my own righteousness, but this time it was a religious "Christian" righteousness, an identity of being the good son. I was just as enslaved to the Law when I was rebelling against it as when I was trying to follow it on my own strength.

You might say I switched from being the immoral woman to being Simon the Pharisee. And I became more loveless, more fearful, more driven, and more demanding. More *exhausted*. We'll look a bit more closely at this tendency in the next chapter, but suffice it to say, it is no wonder that so many Christians who experience this kind of boot-camp mentality in the church walk away altogether.

GOD DOESN'T NEED OUR GOOD WORKS (BUT OUR NEIGHBORS DO!)

What usually follows the laziness and license objections is a concern that championing the cause of unconditional grace overlooks or understates the importance and necessity of good works. This concern revolves around what someone means by "good works" and, more specifically, who are they for? There is a lot of confusion inside the church today regarding these questions. Misunderstanding this issue may be, in my opinion, the primary thing that keeps Christians feeling exhausted.

No one dealt with this better than Martin Luther. One of his most helpful contributions was his distinction between passive righteousness and active righteousness. This distinction was Luther's way to describe the two relationships in which Christians live: before God vertically and before one another horizontally.

Luther asserted that our righteousness before God (*coram Deo*) is received and defined by faith. Our righteousness before one another (*coram mundo*), on the other hand, is active and defined by service. The passive righteousness of faith (vertical righteousness) is what makes us right before God—fully and finally. The active righteousness of works (horizontal righteousness) serves the well-being of creation and culture by loving and serving our neighbors.

This distinction is so helpful because whenever we discuss Christian growth, the doctrine of sanctification, or the practice of godliness, the insinuation is that *my* effort, *my* works, *my* faith, *my* response, and *my* obedience keep me in God's good graces—the more I do "for God," the more He loves me. This, however, undermines the clear biblical teaching that things between Christians and God are forever settled because of what Jesus accomplished on the cross (Rom. 8:1, 31–39; Col. 2:13–14). When we imply that our works are for God and not for others, we perpetuate the idea that God's love for us is dependent on what we do instead of on what Christ has done. We also fall prey to what John Piper calls "the debtors ethic"—paying God back for all He's done for us.

However, when we understand that everything between God and us has been fully and finally made right—that Christians live their lives under a banner that reads "It is finished"—we necessarily turn away from ourselves and turn toward our neighbors. Forever freed *from* our need to pay God back or secure His love, we are now free *to* love and serve others. We work for others horizontally (active righteousness), because God has worked for us vertically (passive righteousness). The Christian lives from belovedness (passive righteousness) to loving action (active righteousness). His love *for* us begets love *from* us. "We are objects of love before we are subjects who love," as my friend Jono Linebaugh likes to say. So, good works and the imperatives that describe them are not called for to establish standing with God, but to serve our neighbors. Life after justification does not eliminate good works, it just "horizontalizes" them.[8]

This is what Paul was getting at when he said in Galatians 5:6, "The only thing that counts is faith [passive righteousness] expressing itself through love [active righteousness]" (NIV). Faith alone, in other words, gives the power to love.

Passive righteousness tells us that God does not need our good works. Active righteousness tells us that our neighbors do. The aim and direction of good works are horizontal, not vertical. So on the horizontal plane—in creature-to-creature relationships (active righteousness)—we can happily talk about effort, action, good works, etc. But it's important to remember two things.

First, it is the passive righteousness of faith that precedes and produces the active righteousness of love for others. Or, to put it another way, our active righteousness, which plays out horizontally, is the fruit of our passive righteousness we are given from God, vertically.

Second, and this is extremely important, our hearts work like magnets that always draw the horizontal (nonsaving) plane toward the vertical. Like a car with bad wheel alignment, we will naturally veer toward viewing our good works as a way of keeping things settled with God on the vertical plane rather than as a way of serving our neighbors on the horizontal. So while we never want to eschew talking about and praising the works of faith-fueled service that spring out of a forgiven heart, we err on the side of emphasizing the passive righteousness that inspires such works.

DISCIPLINED ABOUT DISCIPLINISM

You might ask, "What about the seemingly vertical work of spiritual disciplines? Aren't practices like prayer, Bible reading, going to church, etc., a work that is directed to God? And what about fighting sin in our lives? Isn't that an ongoing work intended to keep God pleased with us?" These are important questions.

Many Christians have assumed (and have been taught!) that Bible reading, prayer, etc., is the way to keep God happy with us—that the more we pray and read our Bibles, the more He will love us. Consciously or not, we often do these things to maintain God's favor. Such reasoning, whether explicitly taught or implicitly caught, could not be more mistaken or toxic! We read the Bible and pray and go to church and partake of the sacraments, because it is in those places that God reminds us that things between Him and us are forever fixed. They are the rendezvous points where God declares to us concretely that the debt has been paid, the ledger put away, and everything we need, in Christ we already possess.

Moreover, when we read the Bible and go to church, pray, etc., we hear descriptions of what loving our neighbors actually looks like on the ground of everyday life. Liberated from the burden and bondage of using the Law to establish our righteousness before God, Christians can look to imperatives not as conditions that have to be met but as helpful descriptions and directions for serving one's neighbor. The Law, in other words, norms neighbor love—it shows us what to do and how to do it. Once a person is emancipated from the natural delusion that keeping the rules makes us right with God, and in faith believes the counterintuitive reality that being made righteous by God's forgiving word precedes and produces loving action, then the justified person is unlocked to love. In his hymn "Jesus Christ Our Savior," Martin Luther put it this way: "Fruit of faith therein be showing that thou art to others loving; to thy neighbor thou wilt do as God in love hath done to you."

If we fail to read our Bibles and pray and so on in this spirit, we will turn even those things—good things!—into self-salvation projects. In fact, we might turn them into self-salvation projects anyway. Praise God that His mercy extends even to those of us who fail to integrate it.

The same reasoning applies to how we fight sin and resist temptation. Sin and temptation are always self-centered after all, or as Augustine put it, "mankind turned in on himself." Failing to believe that everything we need we already have in Christ, we look under every worldly rock and behind every worldly tree for something to make us happy, something to save us, something to set us free. The works of the flesh—"sexual immorality, impurity, sensuality, idolatry, sorcery, enmity, strife, jealousy, fits of anger, rivalries, dissensions, divisions, envy, drunkenness, orgies, and things like these" (Gal. 5:19–21)—are simply the fruit of our attempts to save ourselves.

When Jesus was asked in John 6:28, "What must we do, to be doing the works of God?" he answered, "This is the work of God, that you believe in him whom he has sent." Jesus was making the indisputable point that unbelief is the force that gives birth to all of our bad behavior and every moral failure and the pain and heartbreak those things cause. In his preface to his commentary on Romans, Martin Luther writes:

> … only unbelief is called sin by Christ, as he says in John, chapter 16, "The Spirit will punish the world because of sin, because it does not believe in me." Furthermore, before good or bad works happen—which are the good or bad fruits of the heart—there has to be present in the heart either faith or unbelief, the root, sap and chief power of all sin. That is why, in the Scriptures, unbelief is called the head of the serpent and of the ancient dragon which the offspring of the woman, i.e. Christ, must crush, as was promised to Adam (cf. Genesis 3).[9]

Disbelief, in other words, lies at the root of self-absorption. Without a belief in anything beyond or outside of us, we become so burdened with ourselves that we don't have time to love and serve and give to others. The reason we fight sin, then, is *not* because our sin blocks God's love for us, but because our sin blocks our love for God and others.

So I am all for effort, good works, fighting sin, and resisting temptation as long as we understand that it is not our work for God but God's work for us that has fully and finally set things right between God and sinners.

Still, I would be lying if I didn't say that the older I get, the more convinced I become that the slide toward projecting our horizontal life onto our vertical one is as universal as it is subtle and even unconscious. Any talk of sanctification, therefore, that gives the impression that our efforts secure more (or less) of God's love is a nonstarter that needs to be put to death. As my friend Scott Clark once told me, "We cannot use the doctrine of sanctification to renegotiate our acceptance with God." The good works that naturally and spontaneously flow from faith are not part of a transaction with God—they are for others. Pure and simple.

THE KEYS IN YOUR POCKET

As long as human beings are addicted to their own sense of control, objections to one-way love will never stop. Their precise form may change, but once they stick in our ear, they can erode our confidence in the assurance that is ours in Christ. They can make us forget about the freedom he won for us. Before long, we will find ourselves reenslaved to the Law, running around like mad trying to earn what we already have. But thankfully, God uses even our deluded, furious activity to remind us of His Gospel. He uses our exhaustion! As George Herbert once wrote, from the perspective of God speaking about man, "If goodness lead him not, yet weariness / May toss him to my breast."[10]

As an embarrassing illustration, on more occasions than I would care to admit in the past year, I have been late for a meeting or an appointment because I haven't been able to find my car keys. Certain that either my wife or one of my three children has misplaced them,

I have frantically searched from room to room, looking for someone to blame: "Has anyone seen my keys? I'm late for a meeting. Who was playing with my keys? I put them right here on the counter and now they're gone. They didn't just vanish into thin air! Who picked them up? Where are they? I'm late." And right about the time I'm ready to order mass executions in my home, after I've taken that one last look in my bedroom (huffing and puffing, moaning and groaning), I put my hand in my pocket, and there they are. Like a clown who can't find the sunglasses perched on his own head, the keys had been there the entire time.

Every time I tell that story, people laugh. And rightfully so. What forgetful moron frantically looks for car keys that are in his pocket? Me, that's who.

Unfortunately, this is the way so many of us Christians live: searching high and low for something we already have, trying to earn something we've already been given, forgetting that everything we need, we already possess in Christ. Or perhaps it's not that we forget, perhaps it's that we prefer having the "elf on the shelf" keeping track of our every move. It makes us feel safer. We would rather work under duress than live under freedom. Yet this is precisely why we need to hear, each and every week, the basic good news that because of Jesus's finished work, we already have all of the justification, approval, significance, security, freedom, validation, love, righteousness, and rescue for which we desperately long—and look for in a thousand things that are infinitely smaller than Jesus.

Fortunately for morons like me, the moment we finally give up our desperate search is the same moment we hear that still, small voice. Its message is clear: "The keys are in your pocket."

CHAPTER 10

THE END OF TO-DO LISTS

People used to say, half seriously, that when a person turned forty, they were "over the hill." Life would be a downward slope from there on, with your best days behind you. You don't hear that very often anymore. These days, it's things like "forty is the new thirty"—whatever that means—or the tried and true "life begins at forty." Like any birthday, forty is largely an arbitrary marker, the accompanying slogans being more a way to sell corny greeting cards than anything else. So I admit to some surprise at how much that last refrain has been ringing in my head since I hit the big four-oh. In certain respects, life *did* begin at forty.

When I was twenty-five, I believed I could change the world, and I set about that task with all my strength. I was a go-getter. I had plenty of fuel in the tank and wind at my back. At forty, I have come to realize that I cannot change my wife, my church, or my kids, to say nothing of the world. Try as I might, I have not been able to manufacture outcomes the way I thought I could, either in my own life or other people's. Unfulfilled dreams, ongoing relational tension, the loss of friendships, a hard marriage, rebellious teenagers, the death of loved ones, remaining sinful patterns—whatever it is for you—live long enough, lose enough, suffer enough, and the idealism of youth fades, leaving behind the reality of life in a broken world as a broken person. Instead of the constantly moving escalator of progress I thought I was on when I was twenty-five, my life has looked more like Samuel Johnson's.

Samuel Johnson, the great eighteenth-century thinker and writer, documented in his diary his efforts over the years to fight sloth by getting up early in the morning to pray. He wrote:

> 1738: "Oh, Lord, enable me to redeem the time which I have spent in sloth."
>
> 1757: "Oh, mighty God, enable me to shake off sloth and redeem the time misspent in idleness and sin by diligent application of the days yet remaining."
>
> 1759: "Enable me to shake off idleness and sloth."
>
> 1761: "I have resolved until I have resolved that I am afraid to resolve again."
>
> 1764: "My indolence since my last reception of the sacrament has sunk into grossest sluggishness. My purpose is from this time to avoid idleness and to rise early."

1764 (5 months later): He resolves to rise early, "not later than six if I can."

1765: "I purpose to rise at eight because, though, I shall not rise early it will be much earlier than I now rise for I often lie until two."

1769: "I am not yet in a state to form any resolutions. I purpose and hope to rise early in the morning, by eight, and by degrees, at six."

1775: "When I look back upon resolution of improvement and amendments which have, year after year, been made and broken, why do I yet try to resolve again? I try because reformation is necessary and despair is criminal." He resolves again to rise at eight.

1781 (3 years before his death): "I will not despair, help me, help me, oh my God. I resolve to rise at eight or sooner to avoid idleness."[1]

Dr. Johnson's attitude reminds me much of myself over the years. Try and fail. Fail then try. Try and succeed. Succeed then fail. Two steps forward. One step back. One step forward. Three steps back. Every year, I get better at some things, worse at others. Some areas remain stubbornly static. For example, I have it on good authority that I've become a bit slower to make my point in conversations with my wife—that I listen more and talk less (one step forward!). Perhaps I find it slightly easier to let things go, and criticism doesn't cripple me quite as much. I've even been told I've grown more patient and outwardly trusting of God (cha-ching, cha-ching!). But that's only part of the story. As the years go by, the slings and arrows of life are such that I've also become more self-protective and closed off to other people (one step back). More than ever these days, I keep people at bay—I may trust God more, but I trust those around me less than ever (gong! gong!).

Then there are those areas in which there has been no movement in either direction. No matter how hard I try, I still get frustrated by the same things that frustrated me fifteen years ago: traffic jams, unexpected interruptions, long lines, complainers, feeling misunderstood, people who play it safe, and so on and so forth. To complicate matters even more, there's the paradoxical nature of the whole enterprise—which makes it so difficult to write about. Namely, feeling proud of improvement is almost always a sign that we've gotten worse. Yet when we honestly acknowledge the ways in which we've gotten worse, that tends to be a sign that we are actually getting better. Round and round we go. You get the idea.

In his classic treatise on grace, *The Ragamuffin Gospel*, Brennan Manning wrote, "When I get honest, I admit I am a bundle of paradoxes. I believe and I doubt, I hope and I get discouraged, I love and I hate, I feel bad about feeling good, I feel guilty about not feeling guilty. I am trusting and suspicious. I am honest and I still play games."[2] That's the way it is for all of us. That's the way it is for me. Life isn't what I thought it would be when I was younger. And I'm not what I thought I would be as I've gotten older.

If this sounds like a depressing sentiment, it isn't meant to be one. Quite the opposite. If I am grateful for anything about these past fifteen years, it's for the way God has wrecked my idealism about myself and the world and replaced it with a realism about the extent of His grace and love, which is much bigger than I had ever imagined. Indeed, the smaller you get—the smaller life makes you—the easier it is to see the grandeur of God and His Gospel, the more grateful you become. While I am far more incapable than I may have initially thought, God is infinitely more capable than I ever hoped.

In other words, the older I get, the more smitten I become by the fact that God's love for me, His approval and commitment to me, does not ride on my transformation but on Jesus's substitution. Jesus is infallibly devoted to us in spite of our inconsistent devotion to him. The Gospel is not a command to hang on to Jesus. It's a promise that no matter how weak your faith and how unsuccessful your efforts may be, God is always holding on to you. In this light, life is simply the chronicle of God's successes perfectly meeting our failures.

THE END OF TO-DO-LIST CHRISTIANITY

You see, I grew up believing that the whole goal of being a Christian was to be good, to get better, to progress, to become stronger and stronger, more and more competent. Jesus was essentially Santa Claus. He knew if I had been naughty or nice and would only bring me presents if I behaved. I am pretty sure that I'm not the only American Sunday schooler who picked up on this train of thought. "Santa theology" is commonplace, because it is in our nature to be performance-driven when it comes to our relationship with God. We thank God for saving us, for justifying us, and getting us into the kingdom, but then we drift from grace to performance. *Now that I've been saved, my job is to make sure God doesn't regret His sacrifice,* we think. *I needed Jesus to get me in, but now that I'm in, it's up to me to make sure I stay in.*

Perhaps you remember that Kenny Loggins song from the early 1990s, "Meet Me Half Way"? It could be the theme song of much of modern American Christian preaching. The formal name for this heresy—which can be paraphrased in that unfortunate cliché "God helps those who help themselves"—is Pelagianism. "I do my part, and God does His." We are not Creator and creature; we are partners. In this schema, no matter what the intention may be, Jesus is eventually eclipsed, peripheral at best. *We* become the center of the story. Our faith is no longer about Christ's performance on our behalf, but our performance for him. We become the driver of our lives, and Jesus—if he's in the car at all—is in the backseat shouting instructions as we progress on down the road of sanctification. It took a few major setbacks to open my eyes to how false a conception of Christianity I, and many others like me, had unconsciously swallowed.

I have written elsewhere about the painful experience of merging two congregations in 2008–09, New City and Coral Ridge here in Florida. Divisions, petitions, clandestine meetings, public votes, mudslinging, the whole nine yards—it was awful. Yet God used a pretty nasty experience all the way around, one that coincided with the death of my father, to reveal just how much I was relying on the very idols I was preaching against. When the validation and adoration I was so addicted to were taken away, I realized how much I had been depending on what other people thought of me rather than God's unshakeable love for sinners. Like anyone going through withdrawal, it was extremely painful. I was brought face-to-face with the persistence of sin in the life of Christians, both others and myself. I wanted out. I wanted to quit preaching. I wanted to quit ministry. I wrestled with God and lost. Big-time. It took what was one of the worst times of my life to open my eyes both to the reality of who I was and who God is.

As the subtitle suggests, one of the main inspirations for this book was a desire to bring the good news of God's one-way love to bear on the exhaustion that seems to define so much modern life. You see it in the nonstop world of secular performancism, where people are exhausted by the endless demands of a plugged-in existence. You see it in the to-do list behaviorism of the American church, where well-intentioned Christians run themselves and their fellow believers ragged trying to keep up appearances by doing more and trying harder. For many, their experience in church, theoretically a sanctuary from striving, has perpetuated, not relieved, their exhaustion.

In the midst of such draining circumstances, what allows me to wake up in the morning is the same thing that has made this long, strange trip so worthwhile: the Gospel. Specifically, the breakthrough in understanding the Gospel to be just as much for Christians as it is for non-Christians. I once assumed (along with the vast majority of professing Christians) that the Gospel was simply what non-Christians must believe in order to be saved before advancing to deeper theological waters after their conversion. I didn't realize that once God rescues sinners, His plan isn't to steer us beyond the Gospel but to move us more deeply into it. The good news that Jesus paid it all not only ignites the Christian life but fuels it as well. As my friend J. D. Greear puts it, "The gospel is not just the diving board off of which we jump into the pool of Christianity ... it is the pool that we swim in each and every day."[3]

The church's failure to extend God's one-way love to its members has resulted in the burnout and hypocrisy that characterizes far too much American Christianity, not to mention its perception from the outside as a vehicle of control and judgment.

Ironically, this confusion is not strictly a modern problem. It has roots in the human condition—people addicted to their own sense of control—and so it is something that has plagued the church since its inception. Fortunately, it is also something that Jesus more or less directly addressed.

THE PHARISEE AND THE TAX COLLECTOR

The parable of the Pharisee and the tax collector is probably Christ's most famous and confounding deconstruction of behaviorism:

> Two men went up into the temple to pray, one a Pharisee and the other a tax collector. The Pharisee, standing by himself, prayed thus: "God, I thank you that I am not like other men, extortioners, unjust, adulterers, or even like this tax collector. I fast twice a week; I give tithes of all that I get." But the tax collector, standing far off, would not even lift up his eyes to heaven, but beat his breast, saying, "God, be merciful to me, a sinner!" I tell you, this man went down to his house justified, rather than the other. For everyone who exalts himself will be humbled, but the

one who humbles himself will be exalted. (Luke 18:10–14)

For most, if not all of us, the word *Pharisee* has negative connotations. If we are familiar with the New Testament, what springs to mind are those self-righteous religious leaders who persecuted Jesus at every turn, men who embellished God's Law with rules and regulations that fed their sense of superiority. That is why we have incorporated words like *pharisaical* into our vocabulary, which is synonymous with *legalistic* except that it has an even deeper sting to it.

The contemporaries of Jesus would have had much more positive associations. They would have thought of good men—good dads, good husbands, faithful men who were disciplined to the core and committed to keeping the Word of God. These were true Jewish patriots who were highly honored and esteemed for their commitment to God, morality, goodness, and virtue. If you had told a first-century Jew that he was being pharisaical, he would have accepted that as a compliment with humble appreciation.

In this parable, Jesus made it very clear that the Pharisee *was* as outwardly good as he claimed. His problem, much like good old John Fitzgerald Page, was how he thought about his goodness. His pride, in other words. His record really was something to behold, and he knew it. Look again at his description of himself. He lived an outwardly righteous life. He practiced a consistent religious devotion. It was undoubtedly his practice to go up to the temple regularly to pray. He was honest in his dealings with his fellow man, committed to God, family, church, and country. He was the kind of person you would want for a neighbor.

The radical reversal in this short parable—and in the entire narrative of the New Testament—is that Jesus was saying that the "good" need to repent just as much as the "bad." Religious people need to be forgiven just as much as nonreligious people. To tell a Pharisee that he was the one in need of repentance was mind-blowing to the point of nonsense. "Wait a minute, Jesus," his hearers would have responded. "Are you sure you've got this right? These are the model citizens that we've always tried to emulate … and now you're saying that *they* are the ones who need to repent? What?" Think about it. The same thing happened in the story of the woman washing Christ's feet that we looked at in the last chapter.

OBEDIENCE TO THE RULES WON'T SAVE YOU

Please don't misunderstand. Jesus was not attacking the Pharisees for their obedience or holding it against them. He was attacking them because they were trusting in that obedience for their justification; because they were using it as a way to marginalize and judge others; because their outward compliance was more important to them than the heart of the Law: love for God and neighbor; and more damnably, because they thought they could buy God's favor with their behavior, that God owed them somehow.

Luke's narrative gives the intent of the story: "He also told this parable to some who trusted in themselves that they were righteous …" (v. 9). The Pharisees had stopped trusting in God and had started trusting in themselves and their own abilities. They were human beings, in other words, and like any of us, no matter how much they obsessed over their daily record, they could never have earned their righteousness before God.

There is one final wrinkle. We learn that Jesus told this parable not simply because they were trusting in themselves, but because they "treated others with contempt." Their belief in their capacity to be good enough to impress God and other people fueled contempt for those who weren't obeying the way they were.

The connection is not an arbitrary one. Trusting in oneself, believing that righteousness can be attained through hard work and discipline, always leads to contempt for other people. The impetus for right living, to be righteous before God, was the thing that made this Pharisee, and others like him, unrighteous before Him. Why? Because it engendered hatred for their neighbors and disdain for grace. Some might say this same diagnosis applies to Christians today.

What we see here—and just about everywhere throughout the Gospels—is that the immoral person gets the Gospel before the moral one does. The prostitute understands grace while the Pharisee doesn't. It is the actively unrighteous younger brother who grasps it before his self-righteous older brother. Our goodness is just as toxic as our badness, maybe even more so.

Back to the parable.

A WELL-DESERVED BAD REPUTATION

The tax collector really was as bad as he thought he was. As we noted earlier, tax collectors were essentially debauched thugs and thieving traitors. At some point in this tax collector's life, his love of money had overcome his allegiance to his brothers and sisters, and he had betrayed them.

Jesus wasn't setting him up as someone to be emulated. Jesus exalted this man because he did not even dare to lift up his eyes, instead beating his breast and crying, "God, be merciful to me, a sinner!"

Undoubtedly, when Jesus's audience heard this prayer, they scoffed and said, "Of course he's a sinner! That's the understatement of the century!" But because he knew that he had nothing to bring to the table, righteousness-wise, he went away justified. With empty hands, he could receive the free gift of grace.

Again, sinners love and value grace simply because they know they need it! The self-righteous good man who is impressed with himself is the one who chafes against God's free gift. This is no coincidence. Those who think they are "good" are, in fact, the ones most in need of grace—and the most opposed to it. Yet the whole point of this parable is to demonstrate that Christ has come to bless those who know they are bad and not those who think they are good.

To put it another way, Jesus did not come to offer moral reformation, he came to effect a mortal resurrection. Which is precisely what all of us need—both the "bad people" who know they're bad and the "good people" who think they're good. All of us have fallen short of the glory of God. The Law levels the playing field.

If you're simply looking for moral reformation (improved behavior), you might need a life coach, a cheerleading section, or a really good friend, but not a Savior. But if you require mortal resurrection, you're going to need something beyond yourself, someone who will raise dead people to life, give sight to the blind, and set captives free.

Jesus uses this parable to tell those of us who think we have it together, who never miss work or church, who love our kids and take our wives out on dates, who read our Bibles each morning, that we are still needy beggars who find acceptance with God in Christ's righteousness *alone. Alone!* We never outgrow our need for grace—ever.

HOW TO LOSE FRIENDS AND ALIENATE PEOPLE

If you ever want to clear out a dinner party, bring up the subject of total depravity. The crowd will part like the Red Sea! Yet as unattractive as it sounds, the doctrine of total depravity is not only one of the more misunderstood aspects of Christian theology, it is also one of the most crucial, especially if we are to understand ourselves as creatures whose reliance on God's grace knows no end. So before the Darth Vader theme starts playing in your head, a few notes about what total depravity isn't.

Total depravity does *not* mean "utter depravity." Utter depravity describes someone who is as bad as he or she can possibly be. Thankfully, God's restraining grace keeps even the worst of us from being utterly depraved. Even the most detestable villains of human history could have been worse. So don't read utter depravity into total depravity.

If total depravity isn't utter depravity, then what is it?

As understood and articulated by theologians for centuries, the idea of total depravity means more than one thing. On the one hand, total depravity affirms that we are all born "dead in [our] trespasses and sins" (Eph. 2:1–3; Col. 2:13), with no spiritual capacity to incline ourselves toward God. We do not come into this world spiritually neutral, in other words; we are born with an inheritance of Adam's sin—that is, a death sentence. We therefore need much more than to reach out from our spiritual hospital bed to take the medicine that God offers. We must be raised from death to life. In this sense, total depravity means we are totally unable to approach God on our own power. We will not, because we cannot, and we cannot, because we're dead. In Romans, the apostle Paul puts it like this:

> None is righteous, no, not one;
>> no one understands;
>> no one seeks for God.
> All have turned aside; together they have become
>> worthless;
>> no one does good,
>> not even one. (Rom. 3:10–12)

> For the mind that is set on the flesh is hostile to God, for it does not submit to God's law; indeed, it cannot. Those who are in the flesh cannot please God. (Rom. 8:7–8)

Salvation is not a matter of our coming to God. It is a matter of God coming to us. Robert Capon explains it in this way:

> Jesus came to raise the dead. The only qualification for the gift of the Gospel is to be dead. You don't

have to be smart. You don't have to be good. You
don't have to be wise. You don't have to be wonderful. You just have to be dead. That's it.[4]

So in the sense above, Christians are obviously *not* totally
depraved. We who were dead have been made alive.

> But God, being rich in mercy, because of the great
> love with which he loved us, even when we were
> dead in our trespasses, made us alive together with
> Christ—by grace you have been saved—and raised
> us up with him and seated us with him in the heav-
> enly places in Christ Jesus. (Eph. 2:4–6)

Once God regenerates us by His Spirit, draws us to Himself,
unites us to Christ, raises us from the dead, and grants us status as
adopted sons and daughters, is there *any* sense in which we can speak
of a Christian being totally depraved? Well, yes.

When theologians speak of total depravity, they are not only
referring to our total inability to come to God on our own, but
also to *sin's effect*: sin corrupts us in the totality of our being. Our
minds are affected by sin. Our hearts are affected by sin. Our wills
are affected by sin. Our bodies are affected by sin. This reality
lies at the center of the internal conflict that Paul articulates in
Romans 7:15: "For I do not do what I want, but I do the very
thing I hate."

The painful struggle to which Paul is giving voice arises from his
condition as someone who has been raised from the dead and is now

alive to Christ (justified before God), but lingering sin continues to plague him at every level and in every way (sinful in himself). Paul's testimony demonstrates that even after God saves us, there is no part of us that becomes sin-free—we remain sinful and imperfect in all of our capacities, in the totality of our being, or, as William Beveridge put it:

> I cannot pray but I sin. I cannot hear or preach a
> sermon but I sin. I cannot give alms or receive the
> sacrament but I sin. I can't so much as confess my
> sins, but my confessions are further aggravations
> of them. My repentance needs to be repented of,
> my tears need washing, and the very washing of my
> tears needs still to be washed over again with the
> blood of my Redeemer.[5]

So even after we become Christians, our thoughts, words, motives, deeds, and affections need the constant cleansing of Christ's blood and the forgiveness that comes our way for free. While it is gloriously true that there is nowhere in your life the Spirit has not infiltrated, it is equally true that there is no part of any Christian in this life that is free of sin. Because of the totality of sin's effect, therefore, we never outgrow our need for Christ's finished work on our behalf—we never graduate beyond our desperate need for Christ's righteousness and his strong and perfect blood-soaked plea "before the throne of God above."

This is why the Gospel is just as much for Christians as it is for non-Christians. Our dire need for God's grace doesn't get smaller after God saves us. In one sense, it actually gets bigger. Christian growth, says the apostle Peter, is always growth into grace, not away from it.

So Christian growth does not involve becoming stronger and stronger, more and more competent every day. It involves becoming more and more aware of how weak and incompetent we are and how strong and competent Jesus was and continues to be for us.

Remember, the apostle Paul referred to himself as the least of all the saints and the chief of sinners at the *end* of his life. For Paul, spiritual growth had to do with the realization of how utterly dependent he was on the mercy and grace of God. He did not arrive at some point where he needed Jesus less. It was, paradoxically, Paul's ability to freely admit his lack of sanctification that demonstrated just how sanctified he was. When we stop narcissistically focusing on our need to get better, that *is* what it means to get better. When we stop obsessing over our need to improve, that *is* what it means to improve!

Because of total depravity, you and I were desperate for God's grace before we were saved. Because of total depravity, you and I remain desperate for God's grace even after we're saved. Thankfully, though our sin reaches far, God's grace reaches infinitely further.

SINFUL SAINTS AND SAINTLY SINNERS

At this point someone might say, "Wait a minute. Is *sinner* an appropriate term to describe a Christian's identity? After all, didn't Paul refer to Christians as saints? Once God saves us, aren't we new creatures? The old (sinner) is gone, and the new (saint) has come?" These are important questions.

Once again Martin Luther is a great help to us. He is the one who first described Christians as being *simul justus et peccator* (simultaneously justified and sinner). *Simultaneously* is a crucial word in Christian theology; it describes life and reality "in between the times"—between Jesus's first and second coming, the time after Jesus's bodily resurrection yet before our bodily resurrection. It points to the coexistence of two times at the same time: the old age and the new creation are both present realities. In themselves, Christians remain the old Adam in the old age; in Christ, they share the status of the second Adam (Jesus) in the age to come. *Simul justus et peccator* is a way of identifying this double existence.

The point is not that everyone's a little of each. *Just* and *sinner* are total rather than partial realities. The Christian, in him- or herself, is totally a sinner while at the same time, in Christ, being totally righteous before God. In other words, Christians are fully human—real people with real problems and real pain—who are nevertheless fully known, loved, and saved (Rom. 5:6–10).

The designation of *sinner* is misapplied only if it is used to describe the Christian's core *identity*—their person. Before God, identity is *not* a both/and (sinner *and* saint); it is an either/or (sinner *or* saint). The basis of this difference is not anthropological (what I do or don't do). It is strictly and solely Christological: to be in Christ is to be righteous before God.

Paul does something unprecedented (in comparison with early Jewish literature) in that he designates all people outside of Christ with the identity *sinner* (Rom. 5:8, for example). But even more novel and scandalous is his corresponding claim that it is precisely sinners who are, in Christ, identified as freely justified (Rom. 3:23–24). Sinners and saints at the same time, in other words! So to borrow an expression from a Reformation confession, while the old Adam is a "stubborn, recalcitrant donkey," this does not define Christian identity before God.

So, *simul justus et peccator* is *not* a description of our Christian identity; it is *not* a description of who we are before God. It is, however, a description of the both/and that characterizes the Christian life *as lived* here and now, in the real world.

Pastorally, and in our relationships with other people, this truth allows us to affirm (without crossing our fingers) that in Christ—at the level of identity—the Christian is 100 percent righteous before God, while at the same time recognizing the persistence of sin. If we don't speak in terms of two total states (100 percent righteous in Christ and 100 percent sinful in ourselves) corresponding to the coexistence of two times (the old age and the new creation), then the undeniable reality of ongoing sin leads to the qualification of our identity in Christ: some sin must mean not totally righteous—akin to pouring acid on the very foundation of the peace we have with God on the other side of justification.

If you're a Christian, here's the good news: Who you *really* are has nothing to do with you—how much you can accomplish, who you can become, your behavior (good or bad), your strengths, your weaknesses, your sordid past, your family background, your education, your looks, and so on. Your identity is firmly anchored in Christ's accomplishment, not yours; his strength, not yours; his performance, not yours; his victory, not yours. Your identity is steadfastly established in his substitution, not your sin.

I know all of that might seem a bit technical and overly abstract, but it has been absolutely crucial for me. The distinction between who I am before God (a beloved child and saint) and what my life feels like here and now (a failing sinner) gives me both the assurance that I am loved and accepted by God, as well as the courage to be honest about my ongoing struggles and failures. In other words, I can live my life with hope and without hiding.

The late Brennan Manning put this better than I ever could when he wrote, "To live by grace means to acknowledge my whole life story, the light side and the dark. In admitting my shadow side I learn who I am and what God's grace means.... My deepest awareness of myself is that I am deeply loved by Jesus Christ and I have done nothing to earn it or deserve it."[6] And elsewhere, "Define yourself radically as one beloved by God. This is the true self. Every other identity is illusion."[7] Amen!

CLOSING UP SHOP

I opened this chapter with a reflection on how getting older has dramatically changed the way I understand myself and my faith, especially how I relate, as an individual, to God. What better way to close it than with a comment on how we relate, as a body, to God in light of the incredibly good news that God has done for us—and continues to do for us—what we cannot do for ourselves. If we bring nothing to the table—if all is grace—then our collective hope and mission in life is as hopeful as it is radical. I'll give Robert Capon the final inspiring word:

What role have I left for religion? None. And I have
left none because the Gospel of our Lord and Savior
Jesus Christ leaves none. Christianity is not a religion; it is the announcement of the end of religion.

Religion consists of all the things (believing,
behaving, worshipping, sacrificing) the human
race has ever thought it had to do to get right with
God.… Everything religion tried (and failed) to
do has been perfectly done, once and for all, by
Jesus in his death and resurrection. For Christians,
therefore, the entire religion shop has been closed,
boarded up, and forgotten. The church is not in the
religion business. It never has been and it never will
be, in spite of all the ecclesiastical turkeys through
two thousand years who have acted as if religion
was their stock in trade. The church, instead, is in
the Gospel-proclaiming business. It is not here to
bring the world the bad news that God will think
kindly about us only after we have gone through
certain creedal, liturgical and ethical wickets; it is
here to bring the world the Good News that "while
we were yet sinners, Christ died for the ungodly." It
is here, in short, for no religious purpose at all, only
to announce the Gospel of free grace.[8]

Amen! I don't know about you, but I feel a little less exhausted
already. Probably because the Good News is a bit like this book. It
is finished.

NOTES

Introduction

1. Taylor Clark, *Nerve: Poise Under Pressure, Serenity Under Stress, and the Brave New Science of Fear and Cool* (New York: Little, Brown, 2011), 11.

2. Pamela Paul, "Sleep Medication: Mother's New Little Helper," *New York Times*, November 4, 2011, www.nytimes.com/2011/11/06/fashion/mothers-and -sleep-medication.html?pagewanted=all.

3. American Religious Identification Survey 2008, accessed May 4, 2013, commons .trincoll.edu/aris.

4. "'Nones' on the Rise," The Pew Forum on Religion & Public Life, October 9 2012, www.pewforum.org/Unaffiliated/nones-on-the-rise.aspx#growth.

5. Jerry Bridges, *Transforming Grace: Living Confidently in God's Unfailing Love* (Colorado Springs: NavPress, 1991), 9–10.

6. Max Lucado, *Grace: More Than We Deserve, Greater Than We Imagine* (Nashville: Thomas Nelson, 2012), 45.

7. Robert Farrar Capon, *Between Noon and Three: Romance, Law, and the Outrage of Grace* (New York: Harper & Row, 1982), 114–15.

CHAPTER 1

1. Paraphrased from the introduction insert to Paul F. M. Zahl, "The Merciful Impasse: The Sermon on the Mount for People Who've Crashed (and Burned)" sermon series (Charlottesville, VA: Mockingbird, 2011), 4 compact discs; 6 hrs.

2. Rod Rosenblatt, "The Gospel for Those Broken by the Church," lecture, Faith Lutheran Church / New Reformation Press, audio recording, www.newreformationpress.com /blog/nrp-freebies/the-gospel-for-those-broken-by-the-church/.

3. Paul F. M. Zahl, *Grace in Practice: A Theology of Everyday Life* (Grand Rapids, MI: Eerdmans, 2007), 36.

4. Robert Farrar Capon, *The Romance of the Word: One Man's Love Affair with Theology* (Grand Rapids, MI: Eerdmans, 1996), 10.

5. Robert Farrar Capon, *Between Noon and Three: Romance, Law, and the Outrage of Grace* (New York: Harper & Row, 1982), 7.

CHAPTER 2

1. Brennan Manning and John Blase, *All is Grace: A Ragamuffin Memoir* (Colorado Springs: David C Cook, 2011), 192–94.

2. Reinhold Niebuhr, *Man's Nature and His Communities: Essays on the Dynamics and Enigmas of Man's Personal and Social Existence* (New York: Scribners, 1967), 24.

3. William Hordern, *Living by Grace* (Eugene, OR: Wipf and Stock, 2002), 28.

4. Hordern, *Living by Grace*, 30.

5. T. S. Eliot, "Murder in the Cathedral," *The Complete Poems and Plays of T.S. Eliot* (London: Book Club Associates, 1977), 258.

6. John Z., *Grace in Addiction: The Good News of Alcoholics Anonymous for Everybody* (Charlottesville, VA: Mockingbird, 2012), 67.

CHAPTER 3

1. Wright Thompson, "Urban Meyer Will Be Home for Dinner," *ESPN The Magazine*, August 22, 2012, espn.go.com/espn/otl/story/_/id/8239451/ohio-state-coach-urban -meyer-new-commitment-balancing-work-family-life.

2. Paul F. M. Zahl, *Who Will Deliver Us?: The Present Power of the Death of Christ* (New York: Seabury, 1983), 11.

3. One of the primary problems in talking about the role of the Law is that the term *law* in the Bible does not always mean the same thing. My friend Jono Linebaugh can help us here: "For example, in Psalm 40:8 we read: 'I delight to do your will, O my God; your law is within my heart.' Here the law is synonymous with God's

revealed will. When, however, Paul tells Christians that they are no longer under the law (Rom. 6:14), he obviously means more by law than the revealed will of God. He's talking there about being free from the curse of the law—not needing to depend on adherence to the law to establish our relationship to God: 'Christ is the end of the law for righteousness to everyone who believes' (Rom. 10:4). So, it's not as simple as you might think. For shorthand, it might be helpful to say that law is anything in the Bible that says "do," while gospel is anything in the Bible that says "done"; law equals imperative and gospel equals indicative."

4. Again, many thanks to Dr. Jono Linebaugh for his help with this material.

5. Paul F. M. Zahl, *Who Will Deliver Us?*, 6.

6. Ralph Erskine, *Gospel Sonnets: Or, Spiritual Songs, in Six Parts ... Concerning Creation and Redemption, Law and Gospel, Justification and Sanctification, Faith and Sense, Heaven and Earth* (Glasgow: J. and A. Duncan, 1793), 324.

7. Walter Marshall and Bruce H. McRae, *The Gospel Mystery of Sanctification: Growing in Holiness by Living in Union with Christ* (Eugene, OR: Wipf and Stock, 2004), 117.

8. Thompson, "Urban Meyer Will Be Home for Dinner."

CHAPTER 4

1. Ethan Richardson, *This American Gospel: Public Radio Parables and the Grace of God* (Charlottesville, VA: Mockingbird, 2012), 16.

2. Paul F. M. Zahl, *Who Will Deliver Us?: The Present Power of the Death of Christ* (New York: Seabury, 1983), 22–23.

3. Nick Crews, "'I Am Bitterly, Bitterly Disappointed': Retired Naval Officer's Email to Children in Full," *Telegraph*, November 18, 2012, telegraph.co.uk/news /uknews/9686219/I-am-bitterly-bitterly-disappointed-retired-naval-officers-email -to-children-in-full.html.

4. Rich Mullins, "Testimony," preface to *The Ragamuffin Gospel: Good News for the Bedraggled, Beat-Up, and Burnt Out* by Brennan Manning (Colorado Springs: Multnomah, 2005), 10–11.

5. Jacob Brundle, "Where Are All These 'Loose Women' My Pastor Keeps Warning Me About?" *The Onion*, December 21, 2005, www.theonion.com/articles/where-are-all-these-loose-women-my-pastor-keeps-wa,11190/.

6. Elaine Jarvik, "Utah No. 1 in Online Porn Subscriptions, Report Says," *Deseret News*, March 3, 2009, www.deseretnews.com/article/705288350/Utah-No-1-in-online-porn-subscriptions-report-says.html?pg=all; Julie Cart, "Study Finds Utah Leads Nation in Antidepressant Use," *Los Angeles Times*, February 20, 2002, articles.latimes.com/2002/feb/20/news/mn-28924.

7. Martin Luther, "Commentary on St. Paul's Epistle to the Galatians," accessed June 13, 2013, www.ccel.org/ccel/luther/galatians.iv.html.

8. Luther, "Galatians."

9. Zahl, *Who Will Deliver Us?*, 42–43.

10. J. Gresham Machen, *The Origin of Paul's Religion: The Classic Defense of Supernatural Christianity* (Toronto: Macmillan, 1921), 179.

11. John Dink, "Hallelujah, What a Savior," *Exchange*, May 25, 2012, accessed May 4, 2013, johndink.wordpress.com/2012/05/25/hallelujah-what-a-savior/.

CHAPTER 5

1. Alain Boublil and Claude-Michel Schönberg, "What Have I Done?," *Les Misérables: Cast Recording* (Decca, 1990).

2. Paul F. M. Zahl, *Grace in Practice: A Theology of Everyday Life* (Grand Rapids, MI: Eerdmans, 2007), 38.

3. Richard Rohr, *Everything Belongs* (New York: Crossroad, 1993), 21.

4. J. P. Louw and Eugene Albert Nida, *Greek-English Lexicon of the New Testament: Based on Semantic Domains,* 2nd edition (New York: United Bible Societies, 1996), electronic edition.

5. Victor Hugo, *Les Misérables*, trans. Lee Fahnestock and Norman MacAfee (New York: Penguin, 1987), 76.

CHAPTER 6

1. Based in part on David Zahl, "Robert Downey Jr, Mel Gibson, and the Idiot Forgiveness of God," *Mockingbird*, Nov 7, 2011, www.mbird.com/2011/11/robert-downey-jr-mel -gibson-and-the-idiot-forgiveness-of-god/. Speech recorded by *Telegraph*, telegraph. co.uk.

2. *Wikipedia*, "Bernard Madoff," last modified June 16, 2013, en.wikipedia.org/wiki /Bernard_Madoff.

3. John Tierney, "A Serving of Gratitude May Save the Day," *New York Times*, Nov 21, 2011, nytimes.com/2011/11/22/science/a-serving-of-gratitude-brings-healthy -dividends.html.

4. George Barna and Mark Hatch, *Boiling Point: How Coming Cultural Shifts Will Change Your Life* (Ventura, CA: Regal Books, 2001), 90.

5. Paul F. M. Zahl, *Grace in Practice: A Theology of Everyday Life* (Grand Rapids, MI: Eerdmans, 2007), 36.

6. Sean Norris, ed., *Judgment and Love: Expanded Edition* (Charlottesville, VA: Mockingbird, 2009), 15–16.

CHAPTER 7

1. Emily Gould, "Nightmare Online Dater John Fitzgerald Page Is the Worst Person in the World," *Gawker*, October 11, 2007, gawker.com/309684/nightmare-online-dater -john-fitzgerald-page-is-the-worst-person-in-the-world.

2. Adapted with permission from David Zahl's talk "Grace and (Social) Media," at the 2013 LIBERATE Conference, Feb 24, 2013, liberatenet.org/2013/03/12/watch -david-zahl-at-liberate-2013/.

3. Justin Buzzard, "The Gospel Sets You Free From …," *justinbuzzard.net*, April 8, 2011, accessed May 4, 2013, justinbuzzard.net/2011/04/08/the-gospel-sets-you-free-from/.

4 C. S. Lewis, *Mere Christianity* (San Francisco: Harper, 1952), 128.

5. Osward Bayer, *Living by Faith: Justification and Sanctification*, trans. Geoffrey W. Bromiley (Grand Rapids, MI: Eerdmans, 2003), 25.

6. Walker Percy, *Love in the Ruins* (New York: Farrar, Strauss, and Giroux, 1971), 106.

7. Laura A. Munson, "Those Aren't Fighting Words, Dear," *New York Times*, July 31, 2009, www.nytimes.com/2009/08/02/fashion/02love.html.

CHAPTER 8

1. Referring to himself in the third person in the preface to his book *The Toilers of the Sea*, dated March 1866, Victor Hugo wrote:

> "A triple *ananke* (necessity) weighs upon us: the *ananke* of dogmas, the *ananke* of laws, the *ananke* of things. In *Notre-Dame de Paris* the author has denounced the first; in *Les Miserables* he has pointed out the second; in this book he indicates the third. With these three fatalities which envelop man is mingled the interior fatality, that supreme *ananke*, the human heart." Victor Hugo, *The Toilers of the Sea* (New York: Heritage, 1961), 1.

2. Victor Hugo, *Les Misérables*, trans. Lee Fahnestock and Norman MacAfee (New York: Penguin, 1987), 1322–1325.

3. Alain Boublil and Claude-Michel Schönberg. "Javert's Suicide," *Les Misérables: Cast Recording* (Decca, 1990).

4. Douglas Wilson, "Bones and Silicon," *Blog and Mablog*, November 13, 2010, accessed July 15, 2013, dougwils.com/s12-liturgy-and-worship/bones-and-silicon.html

5. Gerhard O. Forde, *Justification by Faith: A Matter of Death and Life* (Philadelphia: Fortress, 1982), 24.

CHAPTER 9

1. Daniel H. Pink, "Netflix Lets Its Staff Take as Much Holiday as They Want, Whenever They Want—And It Works," *Telegraph*, August 14, 2010, telegraph.co.uk/finance/newsbysector/mediatechnologyandtelecoms/7945719/Netflix-lets-its-staff-take-as-much-holiday-as-they-want-whenever-they-want-and-it-works.html.

2. Tim Keller, "Preaching in a Post-Modern Climate," accessed May 4, 2013, storage
.cloversites.com/citychurch/documents/Preaching%20the%20Gospel%20in%20
a%20Post%20Modern%20Culture.pdf.

3. Michael Horton, "The Fear of Antimonianism," *Out of the Horse's Mouth: Continuing
the Conversation on the Web*, The White Horse Inn Blog, January 27, 2010, accessed
June 13, 2013, whitehorseinn.org/blog/2011/01/27/the-fear-of-antinomianism/.

4. Ralph Erskine, *Gospel Sonnets: Or, Spiritual Songs, in Six Parts ... Concerning
Creation and Redemption, Law and Gospel, Justification and Sanctification, Faith and
Sense, Heaven and Earth* (Glasgow: J. and A. Duncan, 1793), 324.

5. Charles Spurgeon, "Repentance after Conversion," Sermon No. 2419, June 12,
1887.

6. Martin Luther, "A Treatise Against Antinomians Written in an Epistolary Way,"
accessed May 4, 2013, www.truecovenanter.com/truelutheran/luther_against_the
_antinomians.html.

7. JDK, "Big Foot Called My Unicorn an Antinomian," *Mockingbird*, March 23,
2009, www.mbird.com/2009/03/big-foot-called-my-unicorn-antinomian/.

8. Martin Luther described this way of looking at the law as the reality of "living
by faith." Wilfried Joest summed up Luther's thoughts beautifully: "[The end of
the law for faith] does not mean the denial of a Christian ethic.... Luther knows a
commandment that ... gives concrete instruction and an obedience of faith that is
consistent with the freedom of faith.... This commandment, however, is no longer
the *lex implenda* [the law that must be fulfilled], but rather comes to us as the *lex
impleta* [the law that is already fulfilled]. It does not speak to salvation-less people
saying: 'You must, in order that ...' Rather, it speaks to those who have been given
the salvation-gift and says, 'You may, because ...' Wilfried Joest, *Gesetz und Freiheit:
Das Problem des Tertius usus legis bei Luther und die neutestamentliche Parainese*,
fourth edition (Göttingen, Germany: Vadenhoeck & Ruprecht, 1968), 195–96.
Many thanks to Jono Linebaugh for this translation.

9. Martin Luther, "Preface to the Letter of St. Paul to the Romans," trans. Andrew
Thornton, accessed May 4, 2013, www.ccel.org/l/luther/romans/pref_romans.html.

10. George Herbert, "The Pulley."

CHAPTER 10

1. W. Jackson Bate. *Samuel Johnson* (Washington, DC: Counterpoint, 1998), 118–19.

2. Brennan Manning, *The Ragamuffin Gospel: Good News for the Bedraggled, Beat-Up, and Burnt Out* (Colorado Springs: Multnomah, 2005), 25.

3. J. D. Greear, *Gospel: Recovering the Power that Made Christianity Revolutionary* (Nashville: B&H, 2011), 22.

4. Robert Farrar Capon, interview, "Interview with Robert Farrar Capon," *The Wittenburg Door* issue 71, February/March 1983.

5. William Beveridge, *Private Thoughts On Religion and a Christian Life* (Philadelphia: Thomas Kite for E. Littell, 1829), 50.

6. Manning, *The Ragamuffin Gospel*, 25.

7. Brennan Manning, *Abba's Child: The Cry of the Heart for Intimate Belonging* (Colorado Springs: NavPress, 2002), 60.

8. Robert Farrar Capon, *Kingdom, Grace, Judgment: Paradox, Outrage, and Vindication in the Parables of Jesus* (Grand Rapids, MI: Eerdmans, 2002), 252–253.

LIBERATE

𝕏 @pastortullian   @liberatenet

LIBERATE is a resource ministry that seeks to
connect God¹s inexhaustible grace to an
exhausted world through an annual conference,
a website, and a wide range of other media outlets.
To find out more about LIBERATE and Pastor Tullian
go to **www.LiberateNet.org**.

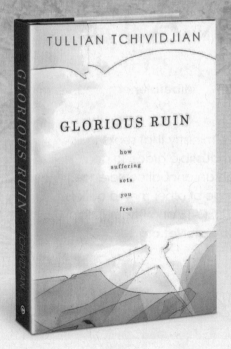

The joy of suffering is not in when it ends but in where it leads.

TULLIAN TCHIVIDJIAN

GLORIOUS RUIN

HOW SUFFERING
SETS YOU FREE

LifeWay
Biblical Solutions for Life

This six-session Bible study takes an honest and refreshing look at the reality of suffering, the ways we tie ourselves in knots trying to deal with it, and the comfort of the gospel for those who can't seem to fix themselves—or others. Learn more online, call 800.458.2772, or visit the LifeWay Christian Store serving you.

lifeway.com/gloriousruin